Wicked Pies Recipes

101 Insanely Delicious and Sweet Pie Recipes

Louise Davidson

All rights reserved © 2021 by Louise Davidson and The Cookbook Publisher. No part of this publication or the information in it may be quoted from or reproduced in any form by means such as printing, scanning, photocopying, or otherwise without prior written permission of the copyright holder.

This book is presented solely for motivational and informational purposes. The author and the publisher do not hold any responsibility for errors, omissions, or contrary interpretation of the subject matter herein.

The recipes provided in this book are for informational purposes only and are not intended to provide dietary advice. A medical practitioner should be consulted before making any changes in diet. Additionally, recipes' cooking times may require adjustment depending on age and quality of appliances. Readers are strongly urged to take all precautions to ensure ingredients are fully cooked to avoid the dangers of foodborne illnesses. The recipes and suggestions provided in this book are solely the opinions of the author. The author and publisher do not take any responsibility for any consequences that may result due to following the instructions provided in this book.

All the nutritional information contained in this book is provided for informational purposes only. This information is based on the specific brands, ingredients, and measurements used to make the recipe, and therefore the nutritional information is an estimate, and in no way is intended to be a guarantee of the actual nutritional value of the recipe made in the reader's home. The author and the publisher will not be responsible for any damages resulting in your reliance on the nutritional information. The best method to obtain an accurate count of the nutritional value in the recipe is to calculate the information with your specific brands, ingredients, and measurements.

ISBN 9798732581898

Printed in the United States

www.thecookbookpublisher.com

CONTENTS

INTRODUCTION

There's nothing like the scent of freshly baked pie in the kitchen, but the days when baking a homemade pie signaled a special occasion are gone. Many of us look back to that tradition with fondness, remembering those pies as the number one comfort food. Those were the days when mom or grandma had painstakingly prepared a special pie packed with love and deliciousness.

It's easy to get a piece of pie nowadays. You can get it pre-baked from your convenience store, or at your local pastry shop or café. There are pre-made fillings and crusts. It's never been this easy.

But those who have baked pies from scratch know the rewarding joy that comes with making one. Some say there is something almost spiritual about baking pies. Every bite of homemade pie seems to impart the maker's love and devotion. This is perhaps why old-fashioned, home baked pies come with so many warm, fuzzy feelings and memories.

The art of making pies starts with a simple buttery pie dough that's easy to make and doesn't require resting or rising. It does require setting a bit so that it becomes firmer and easier to work with, but all that involves is putting it in the refrigerator or freezer. I love the simplicity of making pies. When you have the pie crust done, you are ready to prepare the filling, which usually takes no more than 10–15 minutes. It's always basically stirring the ingredients in a bowl and then pouring the filling into the pie crust.

There are seven different pie dough recipes used as a base in this cookbook. You use them to make different types of pies with different textures.

Pie Crust	Description	Best For
American Flaky	The fat is cut into the crust, to create a crunchy and flaky crust.	Baking the whole pie with the filling, no prebaking required. Best for fruit pies.
Traditional Flaky	Uses lard instead of butter as fat, and a touch of vinegar, which makes the dough less crumbly.	Baking the pie with the filling. Suitable for all types and flavors of pie.
Brisée	No sugar, very flaky, softer than the American flaky pie crust.	Savory pies. Better baked with filling altogether.
Sucrée	With more sugar and softer than the other pie crusts. Usually rolled more thinly than other crusts.	Fruit tarts. Good for prebaking the crust for later use.
Graham	Easy to make, no baking required.	No-bake pies. No need to prebake the pie crust. Often used for cheesecake and squares.
Sablée	Buttery and sweet, this crust has a great crunch.	Prebaking the pie crust before adding the filling. Great for tarts with custards and fruits.
Classic Amish Pie Crust	Simply one flaky and easy to manipulate crust. Lard, flour, water, vinegar, and an egg make this crust which makes the dough less crumbly and simply delicious.	Baking the pie with the filling. Suitable for all types and flavors of pie.

Each pie crust has a different aroma and texture, and you want to use them appropriately in order to achieve maximum flavor. I prefer using the graham cracker crumb crust for no-bake pies because you can make it in advance and store it in the fridge for later use. In fact, all of the pie crusts can be made in advance; they'll last for up to 3 days in a refrigerator or up to 6 months in a freezer. The variation in the different pie crusts comes from using different kinds of fat and sweetener to achieve the desired texture and flavor. For example, the flaky pie crust is when butter (or shortening) is cut into the flour to create a crunchy and flaky base for your pie. It's always best when you can bake this pie crust with the filling rather than prebaking the crust. The brisée crust has no sugar and is very flaky; it's also best baked with the filling in it. Brisée is a French term that means broken, so beware that this crust tends to be crumblier than others. The sucrée pie crust is sweet, full of sugar and butter, and softer than the others. Sablée is a crust where you will get a nice crunch, sweetness, and texture at the same time.

In this cookbook, I have included very flavorful pie recipes that can be made during the whole year, not only the traditional pie season (that is, the fall). On a hot summer day, you want a nice no-bake pie recipe that will chill you out while you are gathering with your friends in your garden. Also, I have separated the pies into 4 categories: fruit-based pies, old-fashioned pies, fun flavors, and no-bake pies. In each category, you will find plenty of recipes that you can make from scratch with any of the pie crusts that you will find at the very beginning of this cookbook. I have given my opinion on which pie crust goes best with every recipe, but you can choose a different one according to your preference. Also, remember that you can always double a pie crust recipe to make a double crust.

You'll find the traditional apple pie and cherry pie here, as well as old-fashioned baked peanut butter pie, maple pecan pie, chocolate pie, and many other pie flavors that are inspired by these classic recipes.

The tools you will need to make a pie are simple, and you probably have them in your kitchen already: a rolling pin, a pie dish, and a mixing bowl to mix the filling and maybe a brush to spread the egg wash for a golden-brown crust. It's that simple.

Usually, pies take quite some time to be fully baked. To be honest, that's the only thing that brings me any anxiety when I'm making pies. It's the hardest part, I know. Even if you are making a no-bake pie recipe, you still need to wait for a couple of hours so the filling can set in the fridge.

To make a perfect pie crust, you need to keep the ingredients cold. If the butter becomes too soft, place it in the freezer so it can set quickly. You can also use ice-cold water to set the butter because when you work it in the dough, it will become soft. Ice water can help a lot here. Another tip when making the pie crust is to handle the dough as little as possible. Every touch softens the butter even more, and the dough will eventually become soggy.

The edges of the crust often get too brown, so you need to protect them in the oven. Just cover the edges with a simple piece of aluminum foil or parchment paper to avoid the dark color. You can also use an adjustable pie crust shield, usually made from silicone and sold in kitchen stores or online. I use foil as it`s easy to just cover the edges of the pie when needed. This helps a lot.

When rolling out the pie crust, dust your working surface as little as possible. If the dough absorbs too much extra flour, it will become tough. And after you're done rolling out the pie crust, brush off the excess flour. You can use a rolling pin to easily transfer the rolled-out crust to your pie pan.

Tips for Making the Perfect Pie

Unlike our grandmothers, we now have the advantage of technology at our disposal. You have the choice to make pies the old-fashioned way, or to use modern equipment.

Following these basic tips will help you create tasty pies with great crusts every time!

Use fresh ingredients in the right proportions

Start with fresh, good quality ingredients to ensure your pie will taste great. The usual proportion is 1:1 for flour to butter and about 1:2 of water to flour by weight. Another well-known conventional proportion of ingredients is 3-2-1: 3 parts flour, 2 parts fat, and 1 part water by weight. Too little butter will cause the dough to break easily and be difficult to handle. In warm climates, butter may be difficult to handle, so shortening may be used, although the resulting crust will not be as tasty. A heaping teaspoon of baking powder to 4 cups of flour can be a big help for the beginning pie maker to achieve a flaky crust.

Keep it cool

The secret to achieving a delicate, flaky crust is to keep things cool. Your flour, water, butter and working surface should be cool. The main reason is to keep your pieces of butter in the dough from melting. The pieces of butter in the dough are what will melt upon baking, leaving layers of flakey crust.

Keep it light and quick

When handling the dough, be light and quick. Be gentle; rough handling will cause the butter and form a solid mass that will give you a tough crust.

Use your hands

Most recipes instruct that one use a pastry blender or two knives to combine the butter with the dry ingredients. The truly old-fashioned way is to rub the butter into the flour with the thumb and forefinger. Butter pieces in the flour the size of half a walnut will give a flaky crust ideal for fruit pies, while making small, pea-sized lumps will make a shorter crust suitable for custard pies. If you have warm hands, run them under cold water and wipe them dry before handling the mixture.

Keep water to a minimum

You only need about 2 to 4 tablespoons of ice water for each cup of flour. A maximum would be about 50% of the amount of flour in your recipe by weight. Too much water will result in a hard and brittle crust. Too little will give a too-crumbly crust that will cause problems in slicing and serving when done.

Roll out the crust

The trick is still to move swiftly. Dusting the tabletop and rolling pin with flour keeps the dough from sticking. As too much flour can make the crust too tough, our grandmas used to line the work table with a kitchen towel and put the rolling pin in a stocking. You can use plastic to line these surfaces. Strokes in rolling should start from the center and go outward towards the edges. Use quick, light strokes. Heavy strokes cause sticking and breaking. The bottom crust should be about ⅛-inch thick, and the top crust slightly thinner. Roll the dough to about 14 inches in diameter and sling it over your pan. Gently press to make it conform to the shape of the pan. Do not stretch the dough as this will lead to shrinkage while baking. Trim off any excess. Roll the remaining dough to make a whole top crust or strips for top.

Give it a rest

Cover the prepared crust with a kitchen towel and and let it rest in a cool, dry area of your kitchen. Or cover it with plastic or foil and let it cool in the refrigerator for 30 minutes to an hour (some recommend 2 hours, with about 5 to 20 minutes of "thawing", or time to allow the dough to soften for easier handling).

This relaxes the dough and ensures the butter does not form a tough mass with the dough. Our grandmothers used to wrap the dough with wax paper and put rice, beans or another pie pan on top of the crust to help it keep its form while resting and chilling.

Glaze with egg white

Brush your lower crust with egg white to prevent the filling from making it soggy when it is baked. Brush more over the top crust to give it a nice, golden brown sheen.

Let the steam off

Pies with juicy fillings need a way to let off steam without deforming the crust. Make several slits in the top crust to allow steam to escape while baking. Some bakers insert dried macaroni into the slits to act like little chimneys while the pie is baking.

The top or bottom crust may be rolled about ½-inch longer than the other. The ½-inch excess can be folded over the other, and the two pressed together to seal. Moistening the edges or using a paste of flour and water can aid in sealing the edges. This will prevent filling from escaping at the sides of the pie. A little cornstarch may be added to the filling to thicken the juices and prevent it from spilling out of the crust.

Blind bake the crust

This means baking the crust on its own before putting in the filling. It can help prevent the crust from getting soggy when baked with the filling, so it will remain crisp and flakey. Bake at 450°F for about 15 minutes; then reduce the heat to 375°F and then bake for about 5 to 10 minutes.

It should just be light golden brown in color, not fully baked. Let it cool before adding filling. To keep the crust from losing its shape while baking, line it with foil and fill it with beans or pie weights. The weight will keep the crust from puffing out of shape due to steam formed in air pockets within it.

For easy clean up

For pies with fillings that tend to boil over, like fruit fillings with juice, place a baking tray underneath the pie to catch any drips and make for easier clean up.

To prevent a too-dark crust

Loosely covering the pie with foil can help prevent an over-darkening of the crust. You may remove the foil during the final minutes of baking to get a nice golden color.

Making pretty pies with lattice pies

To make a lattice top on pies, a woven or interlaced pattern that makes pies look so pretty, it best to use a crust that has a bit of vinegar in it, making it less crumbly. Lattice pie crusts are best used for fruit pies and give your pies a touch of elegance.

To make a lattice pie top, lay the top crust flat on a flour-dusted cutting and cut even strips of dough of ½ to 1 -inch wide. I use a ruler and a pizza cutter for this step. Place half of the dough strips over the pie's filling, in parallel lines, spaced evenly. From the middle, fold over every other strip to the same side. Lay a strip of dough perpendicular to the already placed strips to start your weaving pattern in the middle of the pie, at the fold.

Fold the strips back down over the just placed strip. Fold the other strips that were not the first time over the strip that was just placed and lay another strip of dough at the fold. And continue in this fashion until all the pie is covered. Crimp the edges of the strip with the bottom crust.

Let's get started!

PIE CRUSTS

American Flaky Pie Crust

Buttery and flaky, almost like a puff pastry, this pie crust makes a perfect crust for your pie. It's easy to make and super delicious. Combined with the pie filling, you are going to be amazed how this pie crust makes the best out of your pie.

Makes 2 pie crusts | Prep time 10 minutes | Chill time 1 hour

Ingredients
2½ cups all-purpose flour
Pinch of salt
1 tablespoon sugar
1 cup butter, cooled and diced into cubes
4–5 tablespoons cold water

Directions
1. Place the flour, salt, and sugar in a food processor and blitz until mixed thoroughly.
2. Add the cold butter and blitz in short intervals until you get a sand-like consistency.
3. Pour in the cold water, 1 tablespoon at a time, and blitz until you get a dough-like consistency.
4. Divide the dough into 2 equal parts and shape it into 6-inch discs. Wrap with parchment paper or plastic wrap. Chill in the refrigerator for at least 1 hour before using.

Traditional Flaky Pie Crust

This classic recipe for flaky pie crusts is one of the best you will ever find. The use of lard makes it perfectly tender and flaky at the same time.

Makes 2 pie crusts | Prep time 10 minutes | Chill time 1 hour

Ingredients
3 cups all-purpose flour
1 teaspoon salt
1½ cups lard (such as Crisco or Tenderflake)
2 teaspoons vinegar
1 egg yolk
3–4 tablespoons ice-cold water, more if needed

Directions
1. Place the flour, salt, lard, and vinegar in a food processor and blitz until mixed thoroughly, and get to a sand-like consistency.
2. Pour in the egg yolk and the cold water, 1 tablespoon at a time, and blitz until you get a dough-like consistency.
3. Divide the dough into 2 equal parts and shape it into 6-inch discs.
4. Wrap with parchment paper or plastic wrap and chill in the refrigerator for at least 1 hour before using.

Sucrée Crust

If you're a big pie lover, you will love this French-inspired pie crust. It's sweet and super buttery, and it has a nice richness from the egg yolks used in this recipe. It's perfect for filling with pastry cream and decorating with fruit on top, as well as baking the whole pie or tart together.

Makes 2 pie crusts | Prep time 10 minutes | Chill time 1 hour

Ingredients
3 cups all-purpose flour
½ cup sugar
1 teaspoon salt
1 cup cold butter, diced into cubes
2 egg yolks
2–4 tablespoons ice-cold water

Directions
1. Place the flour, salt, and sugar in a food processor and blitz until mixed thoroughly.
2. Add the cold butter and blitz in short intervals until you get a sand-like consistency.
3. Pour in the egg yolks and cold water, one tablespoon at a time, and blitz until you get a dough-like consistency.
4. Divide the dough into 2 equal parts and shape it into 6-inch discs.
5. Wrap with parchment paper or plastic wrap and chill in the refrigerator for at least 1 hour before using.

Brisée Crust

This all-butter pie crust makes a perfect base for your next pie baking experience. Ready in just 10 minutes, this pie dough is perfect for sweet as well as savory pies. You will love the buttery taste in every single bite.

Makes 1 pie crust | Prep time 10 minutes | Chill time 1 hour

Ingredients
2 cups all-purpose flour
⅝ cup cold butter, diced into cubes
2 tablespoons vegetable shortening
2 pinches of salt
1 tablespoon white vinegar
5–6 tablespoons ice-cold water

Directions
1. Place the flour and salt in a food processor and blitz until mixed thoroughly.
2. Add the cold butter and vegetable shortening and blitz in short intervals until you get a sand-like consistency.
3. Pour in the vinegar and cold water, 1 tablespoon at a time, and blitz until you get a dough-like consistency.
4. Shape the dough into a 6-inch disc.
5. Wrap with parchment paper or plastic wrap and chill in the refrigerator for at least 1 hour before using.

Sablée Crust

If you like your pie crust to be as French as possible, then sablée crust is the thing for you. This makes a perfect crust for pies and tarts as well. Imagine a full, buttery flavor in every single bite while you are eating your favorite pie.

Makes 1 pie crust | Prep time 10 minutes | Chill time 1 hour

Ingredients
1¼ cups all-purpose flour
Pinch of salt
⅓ cup powdered sugar
1–2 tablespoons milk
½ cup butter, cubed
1 large egg yolk

Directions
1. Place the flour, salt, and powdered sugar in a food processor and blitz until mixed thoroughly.
2. Add the cold butter and blitz in short intervals until you get a sand-like consistency.
3. Pour in the egg yolk and milk, one tablespoon at a time, and blitz until you get a dough-like consistency.
4. Shape the dough into a 6-inch disc.
5. Wrap with parchment paper or plastic wrap and chill in the refrigerator for at least 1 hour before using.

No-Bake Graham Cracker Crust

This graham cracker crumb crust makes a perfect crust for your no-bake pie. It is perfect for no-bake projects, but it does go well with baked pies as well. The combination of butter, vanilla, and ground graham crackers is divine and goes perfectly with any pie filling.

Makes 1 pie crust | Prep time 10 minutes | Chill time 30 minutes

Ingredients
1½ cups ground graham cracker crumbs
⅓ cup sugar
1 teaspoon vanilla extract
½ cup butter (1 stick), melted
Pinch of cinnamon

Directions
1. In a large mixing bowl, stir together the ground graham crackers, sugar, and cinnamon.
2. Stir in the vanilla and melted butter and mix until everything is combined.
3. Transfer the Graham-cracker mixture to a 9-inch pie pan and press it down to make the crust at the bottom and around the sides.
4. Chill at least 30 minutes before using.

Classic Amish Pie Crust

Amish are renowned for their homemade pie. The secret of a great pie is all about the crust. Here is the classic Amish recipe for pie crust. This recipe makes 1 crust. Double-up the recipe if you need a double crust.

Makes 1 pie crust | Prep time 10 minutes | Chill time 1 hour

Ingredients
1½ cups flour
½ cup lard
½ teaspoon salt
1 egg
3 tablespoons water
½ tablespoon vinegar

Directions
1. Combine flour and salt.
2. Add in the lard until the mixture forms clumps of small balls.
3. Mix the remaining ingredients and stir into the lard and flour mixture.
4. Shape the dough into a 6-inch disc. Wrap with parchment paper or plastic wrap and chill in the refrigerator for at least 1 hour before using.

FRUIT-BASED PIES

Traditional Apple Pie

Serves 8 | Prep time 20 minutes | Cooking time 55 minutes

Ingredients
1 recipe sucrée crust (page 11)
8 medium apples, peeled and sliced into thin wedges
1 tablespoon lemon juice
½ cup brown sugar
¼ cup vanilla pudding mix
1 teaspoon ground cinnamon
1 large egg, slightly beaten

Directions
1. Preheat the oven at 375°F (185°C).
2. Remove the 2 chilled crust doughs from the refrigerator.
3. Roll out each dough into a thin circle slightly bigger than the pie pan.
4. Place one of the circles in the pie pan, crimp the edge, and cut off the excess dough.
5. In a large mixing bowl, mix the apple slices, lemon juice, brown sugar, vanilla pudding mix, and ground cinnamon.
6. Transfer the apple mixture into the pie crust and smooth it out with a spatula.
7. Cover with the other pie crust and seal the edges of the pie with a fork.
8. Brush the surface of the pie with a lightly whisked egg. Use a knife to make incisions so that the steam can escape while the pie bakes.
9. Bake the oven for 50–55 minutes until the crust is golden brown.
10. Let cool, then slice and serve.

Nutrition per serving
Calories 253, fat 6.2 g, carbs 50.7 g, sugar 35.6 g,
Protein 2.1 g, sodium 160 mg

Apple Crumble Pie

Serves 8 | Prep time 20 minutes | Cooking time 50 minutes

Ingredients

1 recipe sablée crust (page 13)
8 medium apples, peeled and sliced into thin wedges
1 tablespoon lemon juice
½ cup brown sugar
¼ cup vanilla pudding mix
1 teaspoon ground cinnamon

Crumble Topping
½ cup light brown sugar
1 teaspoon ground cinnamon
¾ cup all-purpose flour
¾ cup walnuts, chopped
⅓ cup butter, melted

Directions

1. Preheat an oven at 375°F (185°C).
2. Remove the chilled crust dough from the refrigerator.
3. Roll out the crust into a thin circle slightly bigger than a 9-inch pie pan.
4. Place the circle in the pie pan, crimp the edge, and cut off the excess dough.
5. In a large mixing bowl, mix the apple slices, lemon juice, brown sugar, vanilla pudding mix, and ground cinnamon.
6. Transfer the apple mixture into the pie crust and smooth it out with a spatula.
7. To make the crumble topping, in a mixing bowl, mix the light brown sugar with the ground cinnamon, flour, and walnuts. Stir in the melted butter and make a crumble with your fingers.
8. Sprinkle the crumble on top of the pie.
9. Bake in an oven for 45–50 minutes until the crust is golden brown. Let cool, then slice and serve.

Nutrition per serving

Calories 412, fat 25.6 g, carbs 96.6 g, sugar 15.6 g,
Protein 15.6 g, sodium 415 mg

Classic Apple Cream Pie

Serves 10 | Prep time 8–10 minutes
Cooking time 1 hour 40 minutes

Ingredients
1 recipe sablée crust (page 13)
¼ cup brown sugar
1⅓ cups sugar
¾ cup flour
1 teaspoon grated nutmeg
1½ teaspoons ground cinnamon
1 pinch salt
½ cup walnuts, finely chopped
½ cup butter, cold
4 large peeled apples, cored and sliced
1 cup heavy whipping cream
1 egg
1 teaspoon vanilla extract

Directions
1. Preheat an oven to 350°F (177°C).
2. Remove the chilled crust dough from the refrigerator.
3. Roll out the crust into a thin circle slightly bigger than a 9-inch pie pan.
4. Place the circle in the pie pan, crimp the edge, and cut off the excess dough.
5. In a medium bowl, gently whisk the brown sugar, ¼ cup plus 2 tablespoons of the flour, ⅓ cup of the sugar, 1 teaspoon of cinnamon, nutmeg, and salt.
6. Mix the butter and whisk until crumbly.
7. Mix in the nuts and set aside.
8. Add the apple slices to the crust
9. In a small bowl, thoroughly mix the remaining cinnamon, flour, and sugar.
10. In a medium bowl, gently whisk the egg.
11. Add in the vanilla and cream; combine well.
12. Mix the egg mixture with the cinnamon/flour/sugar mixture from the small bowl.
13. Place this mixture on top of the apple slices.
14. Bake for 55–60 minutes.
15. Take out and top with the nut mixture.

16. Bake for 40–45 more minutes, until golden brown.
17. Take out, cool down for a few minutes, and serve warm!

Nutrition per serving
Calories 473, carbs 64g, fat 24g
Protein 4.7g, sodium 234mg

Perishky Apple Pie

Serves 12–14 | Prep time 15–20 minutes | Cooking time 20 minutes

Ingredients
1 cup lard
5½ cups flour
½ cup butter
1 teaspoon baking powder
2 teaspoons salt
2 cups sugar
1½ cups egg mixture (2 beaten eggs + evaporated milk)
¼ cup flour
7–8 apples, cored and chopped
¼ cup minute tapioca

Directions
1. Preheat an oven to 375 °F (190°C).
2. In a medium bowl, thoroughly mix the butter, flour, and lard.
3. Add the baking powder, egg mixture, and salt; combine well to form a flaky dough.
4. Wrap in plastic or foil and refrigerate overnight (or 3–4 hours minimum).
5. Place the dough on a flat floured surface and roll to form a large circle.
6. Cut using a kitchen knife and make strips 6–8 inches wide.
7. In a separate medium bowl, thoroughly mix the tapioca, flour, and sugar.
8. Place the chopped apple pieces on the strips and top with the tapioca mix.
9. Close the edges and seal.
10. Bake for about 20 minutes until golden brown.
11. Serve warm!

Nutrition per serving
Calories 552, carbs 82g, fat 22.8g,
Protein 7g, sodium 399mg

Apple Spiced Pie

Serves: 8 | Prep time 10–15 minutes | Cooking time 60 minutes

Ingredients
1 recipe sablée crust (page 13)
4 tablespoons lemon juice
8 peeled apples, cored and sliced
⅓ cup sugar
½ cup + 2 tablespoons flour
¼ cup brown sugar
½ cup walnuts, chopped
1 teaspoon cinnamon
½ teaspoon salt
1 teaspoon nutmeg
½ cup butter

Directions
1. Preheat an oven to 375 °F (190°C).
2. Remove the chilled crust dough from the refrigerator.
3. Roll out the crust into a thin circle slightly bigger than a 9-inch pie pan.
4. Place the circle in the pie pan, crimp the edge, and cut off the excess dough.
5. In a medium bowl, thoroughly mix the apple slices and lemon juice.
6. In a separate medium bowl, thoroughly mix both the sugar, cinnamon, flour, nutmeg, and salt.
7. Add in the walnuts and butter; continue mixing.
8. Mix half the cinnamon mixture with the apple mixture; coat well.
9. Pour the mixture into the crust and top with the remaining cinnamon mixture.
10. Cover with foil and bake for 35–40 minutes.
11. Take out, remove the foil and bake for 15–20 more minutes.
12. Serve warm!

Nutrition per serving
Calories 347, carbs 50g, fat 16.8g,
Protein 3.5g, sodium 234mg

Apple Berry Pie

Serves 8 | Prep time 20 minutes | Cooking time 55 minutes

Ingredients
1 recipe sucrée crust (page 11)
4 medium apples, peeled and sliced into thin wedges
1 tablespoon lemon juice
½ cup brown sugar
¼ cup cornstarch
3 cups mixed berries (raspberries, blueberries, and strawberries)
1 teaspoon ground cinnamon
1 large egg, slightly beaten

Directions
1. Preheat the oven at 375°F (185°C).
2. Remove the 2 chilled crust doughs from the refrigerator.
3. Roll out each dough into a thin circle slightly bigger than the pie pan.
4. Place one of the circles in the pie pan, crimp the edge, and cut off the excess dough.
5. In a large mixing bowl, mix the apple slices, lemon juice, brown sugar, cornstarch, mixed berries, and ground cinnamon.
6. Transfer the apple and berry mixture into the pie crust and smooth it out with a spatula.
7. Cover with the other pie crust and seal the edges of the pie with a fork.
8. Brush the surface of the pie with a lightly whisked egg. Use a knife to make incisions so that the steam can escape while the pie bakes.
9. Bake in the oven for 50–55 minutes until the crust is golden brown.
10. Let cool, then slice and serve.

Nutrition per serving
Calories 320, fat 20.6 g, carbs 95 g, sugar 38 g,
Protein 27 g, sodium 156 mg

Peach Pie

Serves 8 | Prep time 20 minutes | Cooking time 55 minutes

Ingredients
1 recipe sucrée crust (page 11)
6 medium peaches, sliced into thin wedges
½ cup sugar
¼ cup vanilla pudding mix
1 teaspoon ground cinnamon
1 large egg, slightly beaten

Directions
1. Preheat the oven at 375°F (185°C).
2. Remove the 2 chilled crust doughs from the refrigerator.
3. Roll out each dough into a thin circle slightly bigger than the pie pan.
4. Place one of the circles in the pie pan, crimp the edge, and cut off the excess dough.
5. In a large mixing bowl, mix the peach slices, sugar, vanilla pudding mix, and ground cinnamon.
6. Transfer the peach mixture into the pie crust and smooth it out with a spatula.
7. Cover with the other pie crust and seal the edges of the pie with a fork.
8. Brush the surface of the pie with a lightly whisked egg. Use a knife to make incisions so that the steam can escape while the pie bakes.
9. Bake the oven for 50–55 minutes until the crust is golden brown.
10. Let cool, then slice and serve.

Nutrition per serving
Calories 261, fat 8.4 g, carbs 45.6 g, sugar 37.4 g,
Protein 3.1 g, sodium 224 mg

Peach and Berry Pie

Serves 8 | Prep time 20 minutes | Cooking time 55 minutes

Ingredients
1 recipe sucrée crust (page 11)
2 medium peaches, sliced into thin wedges
3 cups mixed berries (blueberries, blackberries, and raspberries)
¾ cup sugar
¼ cup vanilla pudding mix
1 large egg, slightly beaten

Directions
1. Preheat the oven at 375°F (185°C).
2. Remove the 2 chilled crust doughs from the refrigerator.
3. Roll out each dough into a thin circle slightly bigger than the pie pan.
4. Place one of the circles in the pie pan, crimp the edge, and cut off the excess dough.
5. In a large mixing bowl, mix the peach slices, sugar, vanilla pudding mix, and mixed berries.
6. Transfer the peach and berry mixture into the pie crust and smooth it out with a spatula.
7. Cover with the other pie crust and seal the edges of the pie with a fork.
8. Brush the surface of the pie with a lightly whisked egg. Use a knife to make incisions so that the steam can escape while the pie bakes.
9. Bake for 50–55 minutes until the crust is golden brown.
10. Let cool, then slice and serve.

Nutrition per serving
Calories 356, fat 19.8 g, carbs 89.8 g, sugar 38.6 g,
Protein 15.6 g, sodium 164 mg

Purple Berry Pie

Serves 10 | Prep time 20 minutes | Cooking time 25 minutes

Ingredients
1 recipe sablée crust (page 13)
3 cups of fresh blueberries
2 cups of fresh blackberries
½ cup sultana raisins
¾ cup of sugar
¼ cup of cornstarch
1 tablespoon lemon juice

Directions
1. Preheat oven to 350°F (177°C).
2. Remove the chilled crust dough from the refrigerator.
3. Roll out the crust into a thin circle slightly bigger than a 9-inch pie pan.
4. Place the circle in the pie pan, crimp the edge, and cut off the excess dough.
5. Bake for 8 to 10 minutes or until the crust is golden brown.
6. Remove from heat, and cool completely.
7. In a large saucepan, whisk together the sugar and cornstarch.
8. Wash the blueberries and blackberries. Stem the fruits if necessary.
9. Place all the berries and raisins into the saucepan and toss until they are coated in the sugar and cornstarch.
10. Add the lemon juice.
11. Place the saucepan on the stove, set the heat to medium, bring it to a boil, usually for 10 to 15 minutes.
12. Remove from heat, and pour into the cooled pie crust.
13. Allow the berry mixture to cool completely before serving.
14. You can serve this pie cold or warm.

Nutrition per serving
Calories 167, fat 4.5 g., carbs 32.1 g
Protein 1.3 g., sugars 19.9 g

Peach and Cherry Pandowdy

Serves 12 | Prep time 30 min. | Chilling time 1 hour | Cooking time 30 min.

Ingredients

For the crust
2 cups all-purpose flour
1 tablespoon sugar
½ teaspoon salt
¾ cup cold unsalted butter, chopped
¼ cup cold vegetable shortening
4–5 tablespoons ice water

For the filling
2½ pounds peaches, pitted, peeled, and sliced, about 8 medium peaches (or about 6 cups frozen sliced peaches, thawed and drained from excess juices)
1½ pounds fresh or frozen (thawed) cherries, pitted
1 cup sugar
6 tablespoons all-purpose flour
1 teaspoon lemon zest
2 tablespoons fresh lemon juice
½ teaspoon salt

Egg wash
1 egg yolk
1 tablespoon water

Directions

1. Combine the flour, salt, and sugar in a mixing bowl, and mix briefly until combined. Cut in the butter and shortening until the mixture has pea-sized pieces. Gradually drizzle in the water just until the dough comes together.
2. Knead the dough a few times and shape it into a small rectangle, wrap, and refrigerate for 1 hour.
3. Preheat the oven to 400°F (204°C), and lightly coat an 11x8 baking or pie dish with butter.
4. Combine all the filling ingredients in a mixing bowl and pour them into the prepared pan.

5. Roll out the dough to a 9-inch square (it will be thick) and cut it into 16 pieces. Arrange the pieces over the filling, overlapping the edges.
6. Prepare the egg wash and brush it over the pastry.
7. Bake for 30 minutes, or until the filling is bubbly and the pastry is golden. Cover it with foil halfway through to prevent over-browning, if needed.

Nutrition per serving
Calories 230, fat 6 g, carbs 41 g, sugar 32 g,
Protein 4 g, sodium 88 mg

Classic Lattice Blueberry Pie

Serves 8 | Prep time 30 minutes | Chill time 30+30 minutes
Cooking time 80-90 minutes

Ingredients
1 recipe traditional flaky crust (page 10)
1 large egg yolk
1 tablespoon heavy cream
Demerara sugar

Blueberry filling
4 cups fresh blueberries, about 24 ounces
¾ cup white sugar
¼ cup cornstarch
1 tablespoon lemon juice
1 tablespoon cold unsalted butter, cubed

Directions
1. Remove the 2 chilled crust doughs from the refrigerator.
2. Meanwhile, prepare the pie filling. Toss together the blueberries, sugar, cornstarch, and lemon juice in a large bowl. Using your fingers or a fork, gently crush some of the blueberries. Set the mixture aside and allow it to soften for 15 minutes.
3. To make the pie crust, lightly flour a piece of parchment paper and roll out one of the doughs to about 11 inches wide. Flip the dough onto a 9-inch pie dish, and press it into the bottom and sides of the plate. Trim off the excess dough, leaving behind about ½ an inch hanging from the lip of the pie dish.
4. Roll out the second piece of dough to about as big as the previous pie crust. Using a sharp knife, cut it into 1-inch thick strips.
5. To assemble, fill the pie crust with the blueberry filling, and shape it into a mound. Place the cold butter cubes in the center of the mound.
6. To make the lattice top, lay 5 pie strips on top of the filling, making sure they are equally spaced. Take a new dough strip and place it perpendicular to the original 5

strips. Take the 2nd and 4th strips and arrange them under the new dough strip. Next, take a new dough strip and repeat the same steps, except this time, place the 1st, 3rd. and 5th strips under the new dough strip.

7. Cover the top with this lattice pattern, and trim off all excess dough. Tuck the dough strips under the pie crust and crimp the edges with your fingers.

8. In a small bowl, whisk together the egg yolk and cream to create an egg wash. Brush the top and edges of the pie with the egg wash and sprinkle some demerara sugar over it. Keep the pie in the fridge for 30 minutes for the pie to firm up.

9. Preheat the oven to 425°F (218°C). Place the rack in the bottom third of the oven.

10. Cover the pie with foil and bake for 20 minutes. Lower the oven temperature to 350°F (177°C), remove the foil and cover the pie with a piece of parchment paper. Halfway through baking, rotate the pie dish and remove the parchment paper.

11. Bake until the dough turns golden brown, and the blueberry filling becomes thick and bubbly for about 60-70 minutes. Remove the pie from the oven and allow it to cool for 3-4 hours before serving.

Nutrition per serving
Calories 371, fat 21 g., carbs 43 g
Protein 4 g., sodium 238 mg

Blueberry Crumble Pie

Serves 8 | Prep time 20 minutes | Cooking time 50 minutes

Ingredients
1 recipe brisée crust (page 12)
6 cups fresh blueberries
1 tablespoon lemon juice
½ cup brown sugar
¼ cup vanilla pudding mix

Crumble Topping
½ cup light brown sugar
1 teaspoon ground cinnamon
¾ cup all-purpose flour
¾ cup almonds, chopped
⅓ cup butter, melted

Directions
1. Preheat an oven at 375°F (185°C).
2. Remove the chilled crust dough from the refrigerator.
3. Roll out the crust into a thin circle slightly bigger than a 9-inch pie pan.
4. Place the circle in the pie pan, crimp the edge, and cut off the excess dough.
5. In a large mixing bowl, mix the blueberries, lemon juice, brown sugar, and vanilla pudding mix.
6. Transfer the blueberry mixture into the pie crust and smooth it out with a spatula.
7. To make the crumble topping, in a mixing bowl, mix the light brown sugar with the ground cinnamon, flour, and almonds. Stir in the melted butter and make a crumble with your fingers.
8. Sprinkle the crumble on top of the pie.
9. Bake the oven for about 45–50 minutes until the crust is golden brown.
10. Let cool, then slice and serve.

Nutrition per serving
Calories 356, fat 20.6 g, carbs 98.9 g, sugar 15.2 g
Protein 19.6 g, sodium 452 mg

Classic Strawberry Pie

Serves 8 | Prep time 20 minutes | Cooking time 50 minutes

Ingredients
1 recipe traditional flaky crust (page 10)
4 cups fresh or frozen strawberries
1 cup sugar
¼ cup cornstarch
1 teaspoon vanilla extract
2 tablespoons butter
1 large egg, lightly whisked, for brushing
2 tablespoons sugar, for sprinkling

Directions
1. Preheat the oven to 375°F (185°C).
2. Remove the 2 chilled crust doughs from the refrigerator.
3. Roll out each dough into a thin circle slightly bigger than the pie pan.
4. Place one of the circles in the pie pan, crimp the edge, and cut off the excess dough.
5. In a large mixing bowl, mix the strawberries, sugar, cornstarch, and vanilla.
6. Transfer the pie filling into the crust and smooth it out with a spatula. Dollop some butter pieces on top of the strawberry filling.
7. Cover with the other pie crust and seal the edges of the pie with a fork.
8. Brush the surface of the pie with a lightly whisked egg. Use a knife to make incisions so that the steam can escape while the pie bakes. Sprinkle sugar on top.
9. Bake in the oven for 50–55 minutes until the crust is golden brown.
10. Let cool, then slice and serve.

Nutrition per serving
Calories 309, fat 9 g, carbs 57.6 g, sugar 45.3 g,
Protein 2.2 g, sodium 133 mg

Strawberry Chiffon Pie

Serves 6-8 | Chill time 4 hours | Prep time 25 min. | Cooking time 10 min.

Ingredients
1 recipe graham cracker crust (page 14)

For the pie filling
1 pint fresh strawberries
½ cup sugar
1 tablespoon unflavored gelatin
¼ cup cold water
½ cup very hot water
1 tablespoon lemon juice
Pinch salt
1 cup whipped cream
1½ tablespoons meringue powder
¼ cup water
¼ cup sugar, divided

Directions
1. Crush the strawberries and stir in the sugar. Set aside for 30 minutes.
2. In a clean bowl, pour the cold water over the gelatin to soften it, and then add the hot water to dissolve it.
3. Add the lemon juice and salt to the strawberries. Stir in the dissolved gelatin.
4. Chill for about an hour, until the berry mixture begins to hold its shape a little when you move it with a spoon.
5. Fold the whipped cream into the berry mixture.
6. Beat the meringue powder with water and half the sugar until soft peaks form. Slowly add the rest of the sugar and continue beating just until stiff peaks form.
7. Fold the meringue mixture into the strawberry mixture, and spread it in the prepared crust. Refrigerate until firm.
8. Top with additional whipped cream, if desired.

Nutrition per serving
Calories 335, fat 8 g, carbs 38 g, sugar 20 g,
Protein 4 g, sodium 104 mg

Strawberry and Rhubarb Pie

Serves 8 | Prep time 20 minutes | Cooking time 50 minutes

Ingredients
1 recipe sucrée crust (page 11)
3 cups fresh strawberries, sliced
2 bunches rhubarb, cut into 1-inch pieces
1 apple, peeled and grated
Zest of 1 lemon
2 teaspoons vanilla extract
1 cup light brown sugar
½ cup cornstarch
1 medium egg, lightly beaten
2 tablespoons turbinado sugar, for sprinkling

Directions
1. Preheat an oven at 375°F (185°C).
2. Remove the 2 chilled crust doughs from the refrigerator.
3. Roll out each dough into a thin circle slightly bigger than the pie pan.
4. Place one of the circles in the pie pan, crimp the edge, and cut off the excess dough.
5. In a large mixing bowl, mix the sliced strawberries, rhubarb, grated apple, lemon zest, vanilla, light brown sugar, and cornstarch.
6. Transfer the filling into the pie crust and smooth it out with a spatula.
7. Cover with the other pie crust and seal the edges of the pie with a fork.
8. Brush the surface of the pie with a lightly whisked egg. Use a knife to make incisions so that the steam can escape while the pie bakes. Sprinkle with turbinado sugar.
9. Bake in the oven for 50–55 minutes until the crust is golden brown.
10. Let cool, then slice and serve.

Nutrition per serving
Calories 289, fat 19.6 g, carbs 29.9 g, sugar 17.9 g,
Protein 2.8 g, sodium 159 mg

Rhubarb Pie

Serves 8 | Prep time 20 minutes | Cooking time 50 minutes

Ingredients
1 recipe sablée crust (page 13)
1 cup light brown sugar
6 cups rhubarb, cut into 1-inch pieces
½ cup cornstarch
2 teaspoons vanilla extract
¼ teaspoon ground cinnamon

Directions
1. Preheat an oven at 375°F (185°C).
2. Remove the chilled crust dough from the refrigerator.
3. Roll out the crust into a thin circle slightly bigger than a 9-inch pie pan.
4. Place the circle in the pie pan, crimp the edge, and cut off the excess dough.
5. In a large mixing bowl, mix the rhubarb pieces with cornstarch, vanilla, light brown sugar, and ground cinnamon.
6. Pour the mixture into the prepared crust.
7. Bake the oven for about 50 minutes until the crust is golden brown and the filling is set.
8. Let cool, dust with powdered sugar, slice, and serve.

Nutrition per serving
Calories 260, fat 20.6 g, carbs 46.5 g, sugar 17.9 g,
Protein 10.5 g, sodium 155 mg

Cherry Pie

Serves 8 | Prep time 20 minutes | Cooking time 50 minutes

Ingredients
1 recipe American flaky pie crust (page 9)
4 cups fresh or frozen tart cherries
1½ cups sugar
¼ cup cornstarch
1 teaspoon vanilla extract
2 tablespoons butter
1 large egg, lightly whisked, for brushing
2 tablespoons sugar, for sprinkling

Directions
1. Preheat the oven at 375°F (185°C).
2. Remove the 2 chilled crust doughs from the refrigerator.
3. Roll out each dough into a thin circle slightly bigger than the pie pan.
4. Place one of the circles in the pie pan, crimp the edge, and cut off the excess dough.
5. In a large mixing bowl, mix the cherries, sugar, cornstarch, and vanilla.
6. Transfer the cherry pie filling into the pie crust and smooth it out with a spatula. Dollop some butter pieces on top of the cherries.
7. Cover with the other pie crust and seal the edges of the pie with a fork.
8. Brush the surface of the pie with a lightly whisked egg. Use a knife to make incisions so that the steam can escape while the pie bakes. Sprinkle sugar on top.
9. Bake in the oven for 50–55 minutes until the crust is golden brown.
10. Let cool, then slice and serve.

Nutrition per serving
Calories 309, fat 9 g, carbs 57.6 g, sugar 45.3 g,
Protein 2.2 g, sodium 133 mg

Lattice Raspberry Pie

*Serves 10 | Prep time 30 minutes | Chill time 30+30 minutes
Cooking time 80 minutes*

Ingredients
1 recipe traditional flaky crust (page 10)
1 large egg yolk
1 tablespoon heavy cream
Demerara sugar

Raspberry filling
4½ cups fresh raspberry
1 cup white sugar
¼ cup cornstarch
2 teaspoons orange juice
1 tablespoon cold unsalted butter, cubed

Directions
1. Remove the 2 chilled crust doughs from the refrigerator.
2. Meanwhile, prepare the pie filling. Toss together the raspberries, sugar, cornstarch, and orange juice in a large bowl. Using a fork, gently crush some of the raspberries. Set the mixture aside and allow it to soften for 15 minutes.
3. To make the pie crust, lightly flour a piece of parchment paper and roll out one of the doughs to about 11 inches wide. Flip the dough onto a 9-inch pie dish, and press it into the bottom and sides of the plate. Trim off the excess dough, leaving behind about ½ an inch hanging from the lip of the pie dish.
4. Roll out the second piece of dough to about as big as the previous pie crust. Using a sharp knife, cut it into ¾-inch thick strips.
5. To assemble, fill the pie crust with the raspberry filling, and shape it into a mound. Place the cold butter cubes in the center of the mound.
6. To make the lattice top, lay 6 pie strips on top of the filling, making sure they are equally spaced. Take a new dough strip and place it perpendicular to the original 6

strips. Take the 2nd, 4th. And 6th strips and arrange them under the new dough strip. Next, take a new dough strip and repeat the same steps, except this time, place the 1st, 3rd. and 5th strips under the new dough strip. Cover the top with this lattice pattern, and trim off all excess dough. Tuck the dough strips under the pie crust and crimp the edges with your fingers.

7. In a small bowl, whisk together the egg yolk and cream to create an egg wash. Brush the top and edges of the pie with the egg wash and sprinkle some demerara sugar over it. Keep the pie in the fridge for 30 minutes for the pie to firm up.

8. Preheat the oven to 425°F (218°C). Place the rack in the bottom third of the oven.

9. Cover the pie with foil and bake for 20 minutes. Lower the oven temperature to 350°F (177°C), remove the foil and cover the pie with a piece of parchment paper. Halfway through baking, rotate the pie dish and remove the parchment paper. Bake until the dough turns golden brown, and the raspberry filling becomes thick and bubbly about 60 minutes. Remove the pie from the oven and allow it to cool before serving.

Nutrition per serving
Calories 359, fat 21 g., carbs 41 g
Protein 3 g., sodium 188 mg

Mixed Berries Pie

Serves 8 | Prep time 20 minutes | Cooking time 50 minutes

Ingredients
1 recipe brisée crust (page 12)
3 cups mixed berries (blueberries, strawberries, and raspberries)
1 cup blueberry preserves
3 tablespoons cornstarch
2 teaspoons lemon juice

Directions
1. Preheat the oven at 375°F (185°C).
2. Remove the chilled crust dough from the refrigerator.
3. Roll out the crust into a thin circle slightly bigger than a 9-inch pie pan.
4. Place the circle in the pie pan, crimp the edge, and cut off the excess dough.
5. In a large mixing bowl, mix the mixed berries with the blueberry preserve, cornstarch, and lemon juice.
6. Pour the filling mixture into the prepared crust.
7. Bake in the oven for about 50 minutes until the crust is golden brown and the filling is set.
8. Let cool, dust with powdered sugar, slice, and serve.

Nutrition per serving
Calories 261, fat 14.9 g, carbs 29.9 g, sugar 18.9 g,
Protein 2.8 g, sodium 155 mg

Key Lime Pie

Serves 8 | Prep time 20 minutes | Cooking time 55 minutes

Ingredients
1 recipe brisée crust (page 12)
4 large egg yolks
1 (14-ounce) can sweetened condensed milk
½ cup key lime juice
1½ cups heavy cream
¼ cup icing sugar
1 teaspoon vanilla extract

Directions
1. Preheat an oven at 375°F (185°C).
2. Remove the chilled crust dough from the refrigerator.
3. Roll out the crust into a thin circle slightly bigger than a 9-inch pie pan.
4. Place the circle in the pie pan, crimp the edge, and cut off the excess dough.
5. In a large mixing bowl, mix the egg yolks with the sweetened condensed milk and key lime juice.
6. Pour the filling into the pie crust.
7. Bake in the oven for 50–55 minutes until the crust is golden brown. Let cool completely.
8. In another bowl, beat the heavy cream with the icing sugar and vanilla until stiff peaks form.
9. Top the pie with the whipped cream.
10. Slice and serve.

Nutrition per serving
Calories 458, fat 30.5 g, carbs 98.5 g, sugar 59.5 g,
Protein 18.6 g, sodium 256 mg

Lime and White Chocolate Cream Pie

Serves 8 | Prep time 40 minutes | Cooking time 50 minutes
Chill time 2 hours

Ingredients
1 recipe graham cracker crust (page 14)
1 egg white
2½ cups sweetened condensed milk
¾ cup pasteurized egg yolk
1 cup lime juice
1 lime, zest
1 lime, sliced into 8 for garnish

White chocolate whipped cream
1½ cups heavy cream
2 tablespoons powdered sugar
½ teaspoon pure vanilla extract
2 tablespoons white chocolate mousse instant mix

Preparation
1. Preheat the oven to 350ºF (177ºC) while brushing the graham cracker crust with the egg white. Cover the crust completely before placing it in the oven to bake for 5 minutes.
2. Whip the egg yolk and condensed milk together until they are blended completely. Add the lime juice and zest to the mixture and continue whipping until the mixture is smooth.
3. If you haven't yet, remove the crust from the oven and let it cool. When the crust has cooled, add in the egg mixture and bake at 250ºF (121ºC) for 25 to 30 minutes.
4. When the pie is cooked, place it on a cooling rack. Once cooled, place it in the refrigerator for at least two hours.

5.   While waiting for the pie to cool, beat the cream, pow-
      dered sugar, and vanilla until smooth peaks form.
      When the mixture is smooth, add in the chocolate
      mousse and beat to stiff peaks.
6.   Spread the white chocolate whipped cream over the
      pie.
7.   To serve, garnish with a slice of lime.

Nutrition per serving
Calories 342, fat 18 g, carbs 34 g, sugar 16 g,
Protein 6 g, sodium 116 mg

Classic Lemon Pie

Serves 10 | Prep time 20 minutes | Cooking time 45 minutes
Cooling time 2 hours

Ingredients
1 recipe sablée crust (page 13)
5 large egg yolks
1⅓ cups water
1 cup sugar
⅓ cup cornstarch
½ cup lemon juice
1 tablespoon lemon zest
2 tablespoons butter, softened

Topping
2 cups heavy whipping cream
1-2 tablespoons superfine sugar
1 teaspoon pure vanilla extract

Directions
1.   Preheat the oven at 375°F (185°C).
2.   Remove the chilled crust dough from the refrigerator.
3.   Roll out the crust into a thin circle slightly bigger than a 9-inch pie pan.
4.   Place the circle in the pie pan, crimp the edge, and cut off the excess dough.
5.   In a saucepan over medium heat, bring the water, sugar, cornstarch, lemon juice, and lemon zest to a boil.
6.   Beat the egg yolks in a mixing bowl. While stirring constantly with a wire whisk, slowly pour in the hot mixture to temper the egg yolks.
7.   Stir in the butter and whisk until combined. Set aside to cool slightly.
8.   Pour the cooled mixture into the prepared crust.
9.   Bake in the oven for 40–45 minutes until the crust is golden brown and the filling is set. Let the pie cool completely before adding the whipped topping, about 2 hours in the refrigerator.
10. To make the whipped cream topping, add the cream to a mixer bowl and beat the cream at high speed until

firm. Add sugar and vanilla and beat just until just
combined.
11.   Spread the whipped cream evenly on top of the pie
before serving.

Nutrition per serving
Calories 336, fat 13.3 g, carbs 50.5 g, sugar 37 g,
Protein 5.4 g, sodium 222 mg

Lemon Chiffon Pie

Serves 10 | Prep time 20 minutes | Cooking time 45 minutes

Ingredients

1 recipe Classic Amish pie crust, pre-baked (page 15)
1½ cups water, divided
½ cup freshly squeezed lemon juice
Zest from 1 lemon
⅛ teaspoon salt
1 ½ cups white sugar, divided
½ cup cold butter
5 tablespoons cornstarch
½ cup water
4 large egg whites
1 pinch cream of tartar
3 large eggs yolks, beaten lightly
Whipped cream for serving

Directions

1. Preheat the oven to 350°F (177°C) and place the oven rack in the middle position.
2. Roll out the chilled dough into an 11-inch circle and place it into a 9-inch pie dish.
3. Crimp the edge, and cut off the excess dough.
4. Poke a few holes at the bottom of the pie crust with a fork. Place in the oven and bake for 8-10 minutes until golden and cooked through.
5. Remove from heat and let cool completely.
6. To make the lemon chiffon filling, combine the water, lemon juice, lemon zest, salt, 1 cup sugar, and butter in a large saucepan. Bring to a boil.
7. Combine the cornstarch and ½ cup of water into a small bowl and whisk until smooth to make a thickening slurry.
8. Decrease the heat to low and add the cornstarch slurry. Stir until combined and let cook until it thickens.
9. Temper the egg yolks with some of the lemon mixture. This involves adding 1-2 tablespoons at a time to the egg yolks and mixing continuously until you get about ¾ cup. Add the egg yolk mixture to the saucepan and

stir to combine. Remove from heat and let cool, about 15-20 minutes.
10. In the meantime, add the egg whites and pinch of cream of tartar to a mixer bowl and beat on high speed until peaks start to form. Slowly add the remaining sugar. Beat until stiff peaks form.
11. Fold in the beaten egg whites with a spatula into the lemon mixture.
12. Spread the lemon chiffon filling into the cooled pie crust. Cover with plastic wrap or parchment paper.
13. Place in the refrigerator for a minimum of 2-3 hours
14. Before serving, add spoonfuls of whipped cream if desired.

Nutrition per serving
Calories 226, fat 12 g, carbs 25 g, sugar 37 g,
Protein 2 g, sodium 125 mg

Lemon Angel Pie

Serves 8 | Prep time 15 minutes | Cooking time 8 minutes

Ingredients
1 recipe graham cracker crust (page 14) or meringue crust

For the lemon filling
5 egg yolks
½ cup sugar
¼ cup lemon juice
Zest of 1 lemon
1 cup

Whipped cream topping
1 cup heavy cream, chilled
2-4 tablespoons confectioner's sugar
1 teaspoon vanilla
1 envelop gelatin to stabilize cream (optional)
¼ tablespoon water

Directions
1. For the lemon filling, beat the yolks until they are thickened, and heat them gently in a double boiler.
2. While continuously beating, add the sugar, lemon juice, and zest.
3. Continue cooking and stirring until the filling is lightly colored and thick.
4. Remove the mixture from the heat and let it cool completely.
5. For the topping, if you are using gelatin, heat the water and add the gelatin, stirring until it is completely dissolved.
6. Let the gelatin cool down a little, but don't let it set.
7. Whip the cream to soft peaks, and gradually add the sugar and vanilla while whipping.
8. Add the gelatin in a thin stream while whipping continuously.
9. To assemble, take 1 cup of the whipped cream topping and gently fold it into the lemon filling.
10. Fill the crust with the lemon filling.

11.   Spoon the remaining whipped cream topping over the filling, and chill.

Nutrition per serving
Calories 335, fat 22.3 g, carbs 29.9 g, sugar 17.9 g, Protein 2.8 g, sodium 15 mg

Lemon Meringue Pie

Serves 8 | Prep time 20 minutes | Cooking time 45 minutes

Ingredients
1 recipe brisée crust (page 12)
5 large egg yolks
1⅓ cups water
1 cup sugar
⅓ cup cornstarch
½ cup lemon juice
1 tablespoon lemon zest
2 tablespoons butter, softened

Meringue
5 large egg whites
½ teaspoon cream of tartar
½ cup sugar

Directions
1. Preheat the oven at 375°F (185°C).
2. Remove the chilled crust dough from the refrigerator.
3. Roll out the crust into a thin circle slightly bigger than a 9-inch pie pan.
4. Place the circle in the pie pan, crimp the edge, and cut off the excess dough.
5. In a saucepan over medium heat, bring the water, sugar, cornstarch, lemon juice, and lemon zest to a boil.
6. Beat the egg yolks in a mixing bowl. While stirring constantly with a wire whisk, slowly pour in the hot mixture to temper the egg yolks.
7. Stir in the butter and whisk until combined. Set aside to cool slightly.
8. Pour the cooled mixture into the prepared crust.
9. Bake in the oven for 40–45 minutes until the crust is golden brown and the filling is set.
10. When the pie is completely cooled, whip the egg whites with the sugar and cream of tartar until very stiff peaks form.
11. Dollop the meringue on top of the pie and burn it with a torch before serving.

Pear Pie

Serves 8 | Prep time 20 minutes | Cooking time 55 minutes

Ingredients
1 recipe traditional flaky crust (page 10
8 medium pears, peeled and sliced into thin wedges
1 tablespoon lemon juice
½ cup brown sugar
¼ cup cornstarch
¼ cup raisins
2 tablespoons rum
1 teaspoon ground cinnamon
1 large egg, slightly beaten

Directions
1. Preheat the oven at 375°F (185°C).
2. Remove the 2 chilled crust doughs from the refrigerator.
3. Roll out each dough into a thin circle slightly bigger than the pie pan.
4. Place one of the circles in the pie pan, crimp the edge, and cut off the excess dough.
5. In a large mixing bowl, mix the pear slices, lemon juice, brown sugar, cornstarch, rum, raisins, and ground cinnamon.
6. Transfer the pear mixture into the pie crust and smooth it out with a spatula.
7. Cover with the other pie crust and seal the edges of the pie with a fork.
8. Brush the surface of the pie with a lightly whisked egg. Use a knife to make incisions so that the steam can escape while the pie bakes.
9. Bake in the oven for 50–55 minutes until the crust is golden brown.
10. Let cool, then slice and serve.

Nutrition per serving
Calories 258, fat 6.1 g, carbs 49.6 g, sugar 28.4 g,
Protein 2.3 g, sodium 117 mg

Pear and Cranberry Pie

Serves 8 | Prep time 20 minutes | Cooking time 55 minutes

Ingredients
1 recipe sucrée crust (page 11)
5 medium pears, peeled and sliced into thin wedges
1 tablespoon lemon juice
¾ cup sugar
¼ cup cornstarch
2 cups dried or fresh cranberries
½ teaspoon ground cinnamon
1 large egg, slightly beaten

Directions
1. Preheat the oven at 375°F (185°C).
2. Remove the 2 chilled crust doughs from the refrigerator.
3. Roll out each dough into a thin circle slightly bigger than the pie pan.
4. Place one of the circles in the pie pan, crimp the edge, and cut off the excess dough.
5. In a large mixing bowl, mix the pear slices, lemon juice, sugar, cornstarch, cranberries, and ground cinnamon.
6. Transfer the pear mixture into the pie crust and smooth it out with a spatula.
7. Cover with the other pie crust and seal the edges of the pie with a fork.
8. Brush the surface of the pie with a lightly whisked egg. Use a knife to make incisions so that the steam can escape while the pie bakes.
9. Bake in the oven for 50–55 minutes until the crust is golden brown.
10. Let cool, then slice and serve.

Nutrition per serving
Calories 256, fat 26.2g, carbs 29.9 g, sugar 17.9 g,
Protein 2.8 g, sodium 15 mg

Apricot Icebox Pie

Serves 8 | Prep time 30 minutes | Chilling time 1 hour | Cooking time 15 minutes

Ingredients
Crust
48 vanilla wafers, crushed
½ cup margarine, melted

Filling
1½ cups icing sugar
¾ cup margarine, melted
3 eggs, beaten
1½ cups heavy cream
¼ cup sugar
½ cup chopped pecans
2 (13-ounce) cans apricot halves

Directions
1. Crush the wafers and mix in the melted margarine. Press the base into a 9-inch pie plate and chill until set.
2. In a medium saucepan, combine the icing sugar, margarine, and eggs. Cook over medium heat, stirring constantly until thickened. Set the pot aside and let it cool a little.
3. Drain the apricots and cut into bite-size pieces.
4. In a separate bowl, whip the cream until it begins to thicken, and gradually incorporate the ¼ cup of sugar. Beat until stiff peaks form. Fold in the apricots and pecans with a spatula.
5. To assemble the pie, place the cooked filling on the bottom, top with the apricot whipped cream.
6. Chill one hour before serving.

Nutrition per serving
Calories 542, fat 28 g, carbs 70 g, sugar 49 g,
Protein 6 g, sodium 293 mg

Raisin Pie

Serves 8 | Prep time 20 minutes | Cooking time 45 minutes

Ingredients
1 recipe American flaky pie crust (page 9)
2 cups water
½ cup sugar
2 tablespoons flour
¼ teaspoon salt
½ teaspoon vanilla extract
1 tablespoon butter
1 tablespoon lemon juice
2 cups raisins

Directions
1. Preheat the oven to 450°F (232°C).
2. Remove the 2 chilled crust doughs from the refrigerator.
3. Roll out each dough into a thin circle slightly bigger than the pie pan.
4. Place one of the circles in the pie pan, crimp the edge, and cut off the excess dough.
5. In a large saucepan, mix the water, sugar, flour, salt, vanilla, butter, and lemon juice together.
6. Stir in the raisins. Bring the mixture to a simmer and cook over low heat for 10 minutes, stirring frequently.
7. Pour the filling into the pastry-lined pie pan.
8. Cover with the other pie crust and seal the edges of the pie with a fork.
9. Bake for 15 minutes, then reduce the heat to 350°F (177°C) and bake 25-30 minutes longer.

Nutrition per serving
Calories 408, fat 16 g, carbs 65 g, sugar 35 g,
Protein 4 g, sodium 325 mg

Oatmeal Raisin Pie

Serves 8 | Prep time 20 minutes | Cooking time 45 minutes

Ingredients
1 recipe sablée crust (page 13)
¾ pound raisins
¾ cup dark rum
1 cup light brown sugar
2 tablespoons all-purpose flour
1½ teaspoons ground cinnamon
4 large eggs, room temperature
1 cup maple syrup
¼ cup butter, melted
2 teaspoons vanilla extract
1½ cups old-fashioned oats

Directions
1. Preheat the oven at 375°F (185°C).
2. Remove the chilled crust dough from the refrigerator.
3. Roll out the crust into a thin circle slightly bigger than a 9-inch pie pan.
4. Place the circle in the pie pan, crimp the edge, and cut off the excess dough.
5. In a saucepan over medium heat, bring the rum and raisins to a boil. Remove from heat and let cool. Drain the excess rum.
6. In a bowl, whisk the eggs, light brown sugar, maple syrup, melted butter, vanilla, and raisins.
7. Stir in the flour, oats, and cinnamon. Pour the pie filling into the prepared pie crust.
8. Bake in the oven for 40–45 minutes until the crust is golden brown and the filling is set.
9. Let cool completely, then slice and serve.

Nutrition per serving
Calories 557, fat 14 g, carbs 93 g, sugar 67 g,
Protein 7 g, sodium 194 mg

OLD-FASHIONED PIES

Chocolate Pie

Serves 8 | Prep time 20 minutes | Cooking time 50 minutes

Ingredients
1 recipe sablée crust (page 13)
1¼ cups sugar
⅓ cup cocoa powder
2 large eggs, room temperature
1 (5-ounce) can evaporated milk
¼ cup butter, melted
Powdered sugar for serving

Directions
1. Preheat the oven at 375°F (185°C).
2. Remove the chilled crust dough from the refrigerator.
3. Roll out the crust into a thin circle slightly bigger than a 9-inch pie pan.
4. Place the circle in the pie pan, crimp the edge, and cut off the excess dough.
5. In a large mixing bowl, mix the eggs with the sugar, cocoa powder, eggs, evaporated milk, and melted butter.
6. Pour the mixture into the prepared crust.
7. Bake in the oven for about 50 minutes until the crust is golden brown and the filling is set.
8. Let cool, dust with powdered sugar, slice, and serve.

Nutrition per serving
Calories 299, fat 14 g, carbs 43 g, sugar 34 g,
Protein 4. g, sodium 217 mg

German Chocolate Pie

Serves 8 | Prep time 20 minutes | Cooking time 55 minutes

Ingredients
1 recipe sablée crust (page 13)
2 large eggs, room temperature
½ cup butter, melted
1¼ cups chocolate chips, melted
½ cup flour
½ cup light brown sugar
1 teaspoon vanilla extract
1 cup chopped pecans
¾ cup coconut flakes

Directions
1. Preheat the oven at 375°F (185°C).
2. Remove the chilled crust dough from the refrigerator.
3. Roll out the crust into a thin circle slightly bigger than a 9-inch pie pan.
4. Place the circle in the pie pan, crimp the edge, and cut off the excess dough.
5. In a large mixing bowl, mix the eggs with the melted butter, melted chocolate chips, flour, light brown sugar, vanilla, chopped pecans, and coconut flakes.
6. Pour the mixture into the prepared crust.
7. Bake in the oven for about 50 minutes until the crust is golden brown and the filling is set.
8. Let cool, slice, and serve.

Nutrition per serving
Calories 489, fat 25.6 g, carbs 42.6 g, sugar 20.3 g,
Protein 12.3 g, sodium 128 mg

Chocolate and Raspberry Pie

Serves 8 | Prep time 20 minutes | Cooking time 50 minutes

Ingredients
1 recipe sablée crust (page 13)
⅓ cup light brown sugar
⅓ cup cocoa powder
2 large eggs, room temperature
1 (5-ounce) can sweetened condensed milk
¼ cup butter, melted
5 ounces fresh or frozen raspberries

Directions
1.   Preheat the oven at 375°F (185°C).
2.   Remove the chilled crust dough from the refrigerator.
3.   Roll out the crust into a thin circle slightly bigger than a 9-inch pie pan.
4.   Place the circle in the pie pan, crimp the edge, and cut off the excess dough.
5.   In a large mixing bowl, mix the eggs with light brown sugar, cocoa powder, sweetened condensed milk, and melted butter. Stir in the raspberries.
6.   Pour the mixture into the prepared crust.
7.   Bake in the oven for about 50 minutes until the crust is golden brown and the filling is set.
8.   Let cool, dust with powdered sugar, slice, and serve.

Nutrition per serving
Calories 261, fat 15 g, carbs 30 g, sugar 18 g,
Protein 3 g, sodium 105 mg

Sugar Pie

*Serves 8 | Prep time 10 minutes | Cool time 30 minutes +
Cooking time 20-30 minutes*

Ingredients
1 recipe classic Amish pie crust, pre-baked (page 15)
1 cup sugar
3 tablespoons cornstarch
1 pinch salt
2 cups milk
2 tablespoons butter
1 teaspoon vanilla
Whipped cream for serving

Directions
1. Preheat the oven to 350ºF (177ºC).
2. Roll out the chilled dough into an 11-inch circle and place it into a 9-inch pie dish. Crimp the edge, and cut off the excess dough.
3. Poke a few holes at the bottom of the pie crust with a fork. Place in the oven and bake for 8-10 minutes until golden and cooked through. Remove from heat and let cool completely for about 30 minutes.
4. Mix the sugar, cornstarch, and salt together in a saucepan.
5. Add the milk and whisk until the sugar is dissolved.
6. Cook over medium heat with constant stirring until the filling is very thick and pudding-like.
7. Remove it from the heat, and stir in the butter and vanilla.
8. Spread the filling in the baked pie crust. Let cool to room temperature
9. Serve at room temperature with some whipped cream if desired.

Nutrition per serving
Calories 506, fat 23 g, carbs 73 g, sugar 33 g,
Protein 4 g, sodium 247 mg

Chess Pie

Serves 8 | Prep time 20 minutes | Cooking time 50 minutes

Ingredients
1 recipe classic Amish pie crust (page 15)
½ cup salted butter, melted
1¼ cups sugar
2 tablespoons cornmeal
1 tablespoon all-purpose flour
⅓ cup whole milk
1 tablespoon white vinegar
1 teaspoon vanilla extract
4 large eggs, room temperature

Directions
1. Preheat the oven at 375°F (185°C).
2. Remove the chilled crust dough from the refrigerator.
3. Roll out the crust into a thin circle slightly bigger than a 9-inch pie pan.
4. Place the circle in the pie pan, crimp the edge, and cut off the excess dough.
5. In a large mixing bowl, mix the melted butter with sugar, whole milk, vinegar, vanilla, and eggs.
6. Stir in the cornmeal and flour and mix until combined.
7. Pour the mixture into the prepared crust.
8. Bake in the oven for about 50 minutes until the crust is golden brown and the filling is set.
9. Let cool, then slice and serve.

Nutrition per serving
Calories 354, fat 19.6 g, carbs 42.1 g, sugar 32.7 g,
Protein 4.6 g, sodium 224 mg

Brown Sugar Chess Pie

Serves 8 | Prep time 20 minutes | Cooking time 50 minutes

Ingredients
1 recipe classic Amish pie crust (page 15)
2 cups light brown sugar
1 cup heavy cream
½ cup butter, melted
1 tablespoon whiskey
2 teaspoons vanilla extract
5 large eggs, room temperature
1 cup all-purpose flour
1 cup heavy whipping cream
2 tablespoons powdered sugar

Directions
1. Preheat the oven at 375°F (185°C).
2. Remove the chilled crust dough from the refrigerator.
3. Roll out the crust into a thin circle slightly bigger than a 9-inch pie pan.
4. Place the circle in the pie pan, crimp the edge, and cut off the excess dough.
5. In a large mixing bowl, mix the melted butter with light brown sugar, heavy cream, whiskey, vanilla, and eggs.
6. Fold in the flour and mix everything into a smooth batter.
7. Pour the mixture into the prepared crust.
8. Bake in the oven for about 50 minutes until the crust is golden brown and the filling is set.
9. Let cool, then slice and serve.

Nutrition per serving
Calories 452, fat 20.9 g, carbs 29.9 g, sugar 17.9 g,
Protein 20.8 g, sodium 453 mg

Buttermilk Pie

Serves 8 | Prep time 20 minutes | Cooking time 50 minutes

Ingredients
1 recipe classic Amish pie crust (page 15)
2 tablespoons all-purpose flour
6 large egg yolks
3 large eggs
1¼ cups buttermilk
1¼ cups sugar
1 tablespoon lemon zest
⅓ cup lemon juice
2 tablespoons butter, melted
1 cup heavy whipping cream, chilled
2 tablespoons icing sugar

Directions
1. Preheat in the oven at 375°F (185°C).
2. Remove the chilled crust dough from the refrigerator.
3. Roll out the crust into a thin circle slightly bigger than a 9-inch pie pan.
4. Place the circle in the pie pan, crimp the edge, and cut off the excess dough.
5. In a large mixing bowl, mix the egg yolks with the whole eggs, buttermilk, sugar, lemon juice, and zest, melted butter, and flour.
6. Pour the mixture into the prepared crust.
7. Bake in the oven for about 50 minutes until the crust is golden brown and the filling is set.
8. Let cool, then slice and serve.

Nutrition per serving
Calories 261, fat 14.9 g, carbs 29.9 g, sugar 17.9 g,
Protein 2.8 g, sodium 15 mg

Mississippi Mud Pie

Serves 8 | Prep time 20 minutes | Cooking time 45 minutes

Ingredients
1 recipe sablée crust (page 13)
½ cup butter
1¾ cups sugar
¼ cup cocoa powder
¼ cup all-purpose flour
4 large eggs, room temperature
1 teaspoon vanilla extract
1½ cups heavy whipping cream
3 tablespoons powdered sugar

Directions
1. Preheat the oven at 375°F (185°C).
2. Remove the chilled crust dough from the refrigerator.
3. Roll out the crust into a thin circle slightly bigger than a 9-inch pie pan.
4. Place the circle in the pie pan, crimp the edge, and cut off the excess dough.
5. In the bowl of a stand mixer, beat the butter with the sugar and cocoa powder.
6. Stir in the eggs one at a time, mixing well after each addition.
7. Stir in the vanilla and flour and mix everything together.
8. Pour the filling into the prepared pie crust.
9. Bake in the oven for 40–45 minutes until the crust is golden brown and the filling is set.
10. Let cool completely and then whip the heavy whipping cream with the powdered sugar until stiff peaks form.
11. Spread the whipped cream on top of the chilled pie and serve.

Nutrition per serving
Calories 423, fat 23.4 g, carbs 53.1 g, sugar 47.1 g
Protein 4.7 g, sodium 139 mg

Honey Pie

Serves 8 | Prep time 20 minutes | Cooking time 50 minutes

Ingredients
1 recipe sablée crust (page 13)
2 cups whole milk
1 cup heavy cream
3 large eggs, room temperature
½ cup honey
⅓ cup light brown sugar
½ cup white sugar
3 tablespoons cornstarch
1 teaspoon vanilla extract

Directions
1. Preheat the oven at 375°F (185°C).
2. Remove the chilled crust dough from the refrigerator.
3. Roll out the crust into a thin circle slightly bigger than a 9-inch pie pan.
4. Place the circle in the pie pan, crimp the edge, and cut off the excess dough.
5. In a saucepan, mix the whole milk and heavy cream. Bring almost to a boil.
6. In a bowl, combine the eggs, honey, and light brown sugar. Slowly pour in the hot mixture, whisking constantly. Stir in the white sugar and vanilla and mix everything together.
7. Pour the filling into the prepared pie crust.
8. Bake in the oven for about 50 minutes until the crust is golden brown and the filling is set.
9. Let cool completely before serving.

Nutrition per serving
Calories 343, fat 15 g, carbs 50 g, sugar 40 g,
Protein 5 g, sodium 161 mg

Sawdust Pie

Serves 8 | Prep time 5 minutes | Cooking time 35 minutes

Ingredients
1 recipe sablée crust (page 13)

For the filling
1½ cups desiccated coconut
1½ cups graham cracker crumbs
1½ cups pecans, chopped
1½ cups sugar
1 cup egg whites

Directions
1. Preheat the oven to 350°F (177°C).
2. Remove the chilled crust dough from the refrigerator.
3. Roll out the crust into a thin circle slightly bigger than a 9-inch pie pan.
4. Place the circle in the pie pan, crimp the edge, and cut off the excess dough.
5. In a bowl, mix the ingredients for the filling EXCEPT for the egg whites.
6. Beat the egg whites just until they are foamy, and stir them into the coconut mixture.
7. Pour it into the pie crust.
8. Bake for about 35 minutes until set.

Nutrition per serving
Calories 439, fat 24 g, carbs 56 g, sugar 45 g,
Protein 7 g, sodium 134 mg

Tyler Pie

Serves 8 | Prep time 10 minutes | Cooking time 35-40 minutes

Ingredients
1 recipe classic Amish pie crust (page 15)
1 cup sugar
½ teaspoon of flour
Pinch salt
2 eggs
1 teaspoon vanilla extract
½ teaspoon lemon extract
Pinch nutmeg
½ cup butter, slightly melted
1 cups milk

Directions
1. Preheat the oven to 350°F (177°C).
2. Remove the chilled crust dough from the refrigerator.
3. Roll out the crust into a thin circle slightly bigger than a 9-inch pie pan.
4. Place the circle in the pie pan, crimp the edge, and cut off the excess dough.
5. In a bowl, combine the sugar, flour, and salt, and mix well.
6. In a separate bowl, beat the eggs and add the vanilla, lemon extract (optional), nutmeg, and butter. Stir in the sugar mixture.
7. Finally, mix in the milk.
8. Pour the filling into the pie crust.
9. Bake until set and nicely brown (about 35-40 minutes).

Nutrition per serving
Calories 422, fat 25 g, carbs 44g, sugar 32 g,
Protein 5 g, sodium 188 mg

Authentic Molasses Pie

Serves 6 | Prep time 10–15 minutes
Cooking time 35–40 minutes

Ingredients
1 recipe sablée crust (page 13)
¾ cup boiling water
¾ cup dark molasses
½ teaspoon baking soda

Top Part
¼ cup butter
1½ cups flour
½ cup brown sugar

Directions
1. Preheat an oven to 375°F (190°C).
2. Remove the chilled crust dough from the refrigerator.
3. Roll out the crust into a thin circle slightly bigger than a 9-inch pie pan.
4. Place the circle in the pie pan, crimp the edge, and cut off the excess dough.
5. In a medium bowl, add the molasses, baking soda, and hot water; dissolve completely.
6. Take a separate medium bowl, add in the flour and sugar and continue mixing.
7. Add in the shortening and mix until crumbs are formed.
8. Pour a ⅓ portion of the molasses mixture into the crust.
9. Top with a ⅓ portion of the crumb mixture.
10. Continue to layer in the same manner.
11. Bake for 35 minutes.
12. Take out, cool down for a few minutes, and serve warm!

Nutrition per serving
Calories 342, carbs 64g, fat 7.4g,
Protein 4.6g, sodium 533mg

Vinegar Pie

Serves 8 | Prep time 10 minutes | Cooking time 35 minutes

Ingredients
1 recipe classic Amish pie crust, pre-baked (page 15)
3 tablespoons flour
1 cup sugar
⅓ cup white vinegar
1 ⅔ cups hot water
1 egg, well beaten
1 teaspoon lemon extract
2 tablespoons butter

Meringue Topping
¼ teaspoon cream of tartar
½ cup sugar
4 large egg whites, at room temperature
½ teaspoon vanilla extract

Directions
1. Preheat the oven to 325°F (163°C).
2. Roll out the chilled dough into an 11-inch circle and place it into a 9-inch pie dish. Crimp the edge, and cut off the excess dough.
3. Poke a few holes at the bottom of the pie crust with a fork. Place in the oven and bake for 8-10 minutes until golden and cooked through. Remove from heat and let cool completely for about 30 minutes.
4. Combine the sugar with the flour in a double boiler.
5. Whisk in the vinegar, water, egg, and lemon flavor.
6. Cook, stirring, in the double boiler until the mixture is thick.
7. Remove from the heat and stir in the butter.
8. Pour the filling into the pie crust.
9. To make the meringue, in a large glass or metal bowl, whip the egg whites until they are foamy. Add the sugar gradually, and continue to whip until stiff peaks form.
10. Pile the meringue topping on the filling and spread to the edges of the pie. Use a fork to create swirls and peaks.

11. Bake until the meringue is golden brown (about 15 minutes).
12. Serve hot.

Nutrition per serving
Calories 325, fat 15 g, carbs 42 g, sugar 26 g,
Protein 5 g, sodium 181 mg

Cream Vanilla Pie

Serves 6–8 | Prep time 10–15 minutes | Cooking time 25 minutes

Ingredients
1 recipe sablée crust (page 13)
⅛ teaspoon salt
¾ cup sugar
2 cups half-and-half
¼ cup brown sugar
½ cup whipping cream
¼ cup cornstarch
1 teaspoon vanilla
½ cup butter or margarine

Directions
1. Preheat an oven to 375°F (190°C).
2. Remove the chilled crust dough from the refrigerator.
3. Roll out the crust into a thin circle slightly bigger than a 9-inch pie pan.
4. Place the circle in the pie pan, crimp the edge, and cut off the excess dough.
5. Take a medium saucepan and add in the half-and-half, whipping cream, salt, and sugar.
6. Heat the pan over medium heat until boiling.
7. In another medium saucepan, mix the sugar and cornstarch.
8. Mix in the cream mixture and stir a little.
9. Add the butter or margarine.
10. Heat the pan over medium heat for 5–6 minutes.
11. Mix in the vanilla and pour in the crust.
12. Top with nutmeg and cinnamon.
13. Bake for 25 minutes.
14. Take out, cool down for a few minutes, and serve warm!

Nutrition per serving
Calories 266, carbs 29g, fat 17g,
Protein 0.8g, sodium 140mg

Cinnamon Pie

Serves 8 | Prep time 20 minutes | Cooking time 50 minutes

Ingredients
1 recipe sablée crust (page 13)
1 cup light brown sugar
2 large eggs, room temperature
1 large egg yolk, room temperature
1¼ cups heavy whipping cream
¼ cup all-purpose flour
3½ tablespoons ground cinnamon
2 teaspoons vanilla extract
½ teaspoon ground nutmeg
Powdered sugar, for serving

Directions
1. Preheat the oven at 375°F (185°C).
2. Remove the chilled crust dough from the refrigerator.
3. Roll out the crust into a thin circle slightly bigger than a 9-inch pie pan.
4. Place the circle in the pie pan, crimp the edge, and cut off the excess dough.
5. In a large mixing bowl, mix the eggs with the egg yolk, light brown sugar, heavy whipping cream, flour, cinnamon, vanilla, and ground nutmeg.
6. Pour the mixture into the prepared crust.
7. Bake in the oven for about 50 minutes until the crust is golden brown and the filling is set.
8. Let cool, dust with powdered sugar, slice, and serve.

Nutrition per serving
Calories 261, fat 14.1 g, carbs 32.9 g, sugar 19.6 g
Protein 3.5 g, sodium 133 mg

Old-Fashioned Baked Peanut Butter Pie

Serves 8 | Prep time 20 minutes | Cooking time 50 minutes

Ingredients
1 recipe sablée crust (page 13)
1 cup light corn syrup
½ cup sugar
½ cup creamy peanut butter
Pinch of salt
4 large eggs, room temperature
Chocolate sauce, for drizzling

Directions
1. Preheat the oven at 375°F (185°C).
2. Remove the chilled crust dough from the refrigerator.
3. Roll out the crust into a thin circle slightly bigger than a 9-inch pie pan.
4. Place the circle in the pie pan, crimp the edge, and cut off the excess dough.
5. In a large mixing bowl, beat the peanut butter with the sugar.
6. Stir in the corn syrup and salt. Add the eggs one at a time, mixing well after each addition.
7. Pour the mixture into the prepared crust.
8. Bake in the oven for about 50 minutes until the crust is golden brown and the filling is set.
9. Let cool, slice, and serve with chocolate sauce on top.

Nutrition per serving
Calories 373, fat 16 g, carbs 54 g, sugar 25 g,
Protein 8 g, sodium 242 mg

Banoffee Pie

Serves 8 | Prep time 20 minutes | Cooking time 5 minutes
Chill time 7 hours

Ingredients
3 cups chocolate wafers or chocolate digestive cookies
½ cup unsalted butter, melted
1 cup caramel sauce or dulce de leche
2 bananas, peeled and sliced
1½ cups chilled heavy whipping cream
¼ cup confectioners' sugar or powdered sugar
1 teaspoon vanilla extract
2 ounces chocolate curls, chunks, or chocolate chips

Directions
1. Grease an 8-inch pie pan with some butter or cooking oil.
2. In a food processor, process the cookies into crumbs.
3. Place the crumbs in a Ziploc bag and crush them with a rolling pin.
4. Melt the butter in a medium saucepan or skillet over medium heat.
5. Add the crumbs and mix well.
6. Add the mixture to the pie pan and press to make a ¼-inch-thick crust. Refrigerate for 4 hours.
7. Melt the chocolate in a double broiler. Pour it over the crust to make a thin layer.
8. Refrigerate for 1 hour more.
9. Use a knife to create curls over the chocolate layer.
10. Pour on the caramel sauce or dulce de leche and spread evenly.
11. Arrange the sliced bananas over it.
12. Combine the heavy cream, vanilla, and icing sugar until well blended.
13. Pour the mixture over the bananas. Top with chocolate curls/chunks/chips.
14. Refrigerate for a final 2 hours. Slice and serve.

Nutrition per serving
Calories 435, fat 21 g, carbs 56 g, sugar 35 g,
Protein 6 g, sodium 302 mg

Soda Cracker Pie

Serves 8 | Prep time 15 minutes | Cooking time 35 minutes

Ingredients
18 soda crackers, also known as saltine crackers
1 cup pecans, chopped
3 eggs whites
1 cup white sugar
1 teaspoon vanilla extract
1 teaspoon baking powder
⅛ teaspoon cream of tartar
6 ripe peaches, cored, peeled, and sliced
Whipped cream for topping

Directions
1. Preheat oven to 350°F (177°C). Grease a 9-inch pie dish.
2. Place the cracker in a sealable bag. With a rolling pin, crush the crackers. Placed the crushed crackers into a large mixing bowl, and add pecans and baking powder. Combine well, and set aside.
3. Place the egg whites into a mixing bowl, and add the cream of tartar. Beat the egg whites on high speed until you get stiff picks. Slowly add the sugar and the vanilla while continuously beating until well combined.
4. Add the egg whites to the dry mixture. Stir with a wooden spoon or spatula just enough to combine.
5. Pour the mixture into the pie dish, and bake 23-25 minutes, until golden. Remove from oven, and let cool on a wired rack.
6. To serve, cut into slices, top with peach slices and whipped cream.

Nutrition per serving
Calories 242, fat 11 g, carbs 33 g, sugar 26 g,
Protein 3 g, sodium 122 mg

Flapper Pie

Serves 6-8 | Prep time 20 min. | Cooking time 10-15 min

Ingredients
1 recipe graham cracker crust (page 14)

For the filling
2½ cups milk
½ cup white sugar
¼ cup cornstarch
3 egg yolks
1 teaspoon vanilla
Pinch salt

Meringue topping
3 egg whites
1 pinch cream of tarter
⅓ cup sugar

Directions
1. To make the filling, in a saucepan, combine the filling ingredients and cook over medium heat, stirring constantly.
2. Continue cooking until the custard has thickened.
3. Allow the mixture to cool while preparing the meringue topping.
4. To make the meringue, beat the egg whites until foamy.
5. Add the cream of tartar and gradually beat in the sugar.
6. Beat until stiff peaks form. Set aside.
7. To assemble and bake, preheat the oven to 350°F (177°C). Spread the filling in the crust while it is still slightly warm, and spoon the meringue on top.
8. Swirl the meringue with a fork and swirl to form peaks.
9. Bake for 15 minutes until the meringue is golden brown.
10. Sprinkle with the reserved crust mixture to garnish.

Nutrition per serving
Calories 481, fat 22 g, carbs 65 g, sugar 50 g,
Protein 9 g, sodium 306 mg

Shoofly Pie

Serves 8 | Prep time 15 minutes | Cooking time 35 minutes

Ingredients
1 recipe classic Amish pie crust (page 15)

For the filling
½ teaspoon baking soda
¾ cup boiling water
1 cup dark molasses
½ cup brown sugar
1½ cups flour
¼ cup shortening or butter

Directions
1. Preheat the oven to 375 °F (190°C).
2. Remove the chilled crust dough from the refrigerator.
3. Roll out the crust into a thin circle slightly bigger than a 9-inch pie pan.
4. Place the circle in the pie pan, crimp the edge, and cut off the excess dough.
5. In a bowl, combine the baking soda, hot water, and molasses.
6. In another bowl, combine the sugar and flour. Rub in the shortening until the mixture looks like crumbs.
7. Pour ⅓ of the molasses mixture into the pie crust, and follow with ⅓ of the crumb mixture.
8. Repeat the layers, making sure to end with the crumb mixture on top.
9. Bake for 35 minutes.

Nutrition per serving
Calories 396, fat 11 g, carbs 70 g, sugar 23 g,
Protein 4 g, sodium 342 mg

Treacle Pie

Serves 8 | Prep time 20 minutes | Cooking time 50 minutes

Ingredients
1 recipe classic Amish pie crust (page 15)
1¼ cups golden syrup
Zest and juice of 1 lemon
1¼ cups white breadcrumbs
3 tablespoons heavy cream
1 large egg

Directions
1. Preheat the oven at 375°F (185°C).
2. Remove the chilled crust dough from the refrigerator.
3. Roll out the crust into a thin circle slightly bigger than a 9-inch pie pan.
4. Place the circle in the pie pan, crimp the edge, and cut off the excess dough.
5. In a large mixing bowl, mix the golden syrup, lemon zest, and juice, breadcrumbs, heavy cream, and egg.
6. Pour the mixture into the prepared crust.
7. Bake in the oven for about 50 minutes until the crust is golden brown and the filling is set.
8. Let cool, dust with powdered sugar, slice, and serve.

Nutrition per serving
Calories 391, fat 11.1 g, carbs 71.7 g, sugar 26.4 g,
Protein 4.5 g, sodium 386 mg

HOLIDAY AND CELEBRATION PIES

Eggnog Pie

Serves 8 | Prep time 20 minutes | Cooking time 50 minutes

Ingredients
1 recipe brisée crust (page 12)
2 cups eggnog
½ cup sugar
¼ cup cornstarch
1 teaspoon ground cinnamon
1 teaspoon vanilla extract
1 envelope gelatin, dissolved in water

Directions
1. Preheat the oven at 375°F (185°C).
2. Remove the chilled crust dough from the refrigerator.
3. Roll out the crust into a thin circle slightly bigger than a 9-inch pie pan.
4. Place the circle in the pie pan, crimp the edge, and cut off the excess dough.
5. In a large mixing bowl, mix the eggnog with sugar, cornstarch, cinnamon, vanilla, and dissolved gelatin.
6. Pour the mixture into the prepared crust.
7. Bake in the oven for about 50 minutes until the crust is golden brown and the filling is set.
8. Let cool, dust with powdered sugar, slice, and serve.

Nutrition per serving
Calories 234, fat 9.9 g, carbs 32.9 g, sugar 18.6 g,
Protein 3.9 g, sodium 139 mg

Eggnog Custard Pie

Serves 8 | Prep time 15 minutes | Cooking time 50 minutes | Chill time 2-3 hours

Ingredients
1½ cups finely crushed vanilla wafers
5 tablespoons melted butter
2 tablespoons sugar
1⅔ cups eggnog
¼ cup chai crème liqueur
3 eggs, lightly beaten
½ teaspoon vanilla
⅛ teaspoon salt
¼ teaspoon ground nutmeg
Grated whole nutmeg

Directions
1. Preheat oven to 350°F (177°C).
2. In a bowl, mix together the vanilla wafers and the melted butter. Press this mixture in the bottom and up along the side of a pie pan and bake for 10 minutes.
3. In a large bowl, blend together the eggs, the eggnog, the chai crème liqueur, the sugar, the vanilla, the ground nutmeg, and the salt.
4. When the crust is done, pour the eggnog mixture into the baked crust and bake for 35 minutes.
5. Let the pie cool for 1 hour. Cover the pie and chill it for several hours before serving. Sprinkle the top of the pie with the grated nutmeg.

Nutrition per serving
Calories 326, fat 17 g, carbs 32 g, sugar 19 g,
Protein 11 g, sodium 255 mg

Southern Pecan Pie

Serves 8 | Prep time 15 minutes | Cooking time 1 hour

Ingredients
1 recipe brisée crust (page 12)
1 cup sugar
1½ cups corn syrup (dark, light, or a combination)
4 eggs
¼ cup butter
1½ teaspoons vanilla
½ teaspoon salt
1½ cups pecans, coarsely broken

Directions
1.   Preheat the oven to 350°F (177°C).
2.   Remove the chilled crust dough from the refrigerator.
3.   Roll out the crust into a thin circle slightly bigger than a 9-inch pie pan.
4.   Place the circle in the pie pan, crimp the edge, and cut off the excess dough.
5.   In a medium saucepan, boil the sugar and corn syrup together for 2-3 minutes, and set aside to cool slightly.
6.   In a large bowl, beat the eggs lightly, and then very slowly pour the syrup mixture into the eggs, stirring constantly.
7.   Strain the mixture to make sure there are no lumps.
8.   Stir in the butter, vanilla, salt, and pecans and pour into crust.
9.   Bake for about 45 to 60 minutes, or until set.

Nutrition per serving
Calories 584, fat 28 g, carbs 83 g, sugar 42 g,
Protein 7 g, sodium 178 mg

Maple Pecan Pie

Serves 8 | Prep time 20 minutes | Cooking time 50 minutes

Ingredients
1 recipe brisée crust (page 12)
2½ cups pecans
3 large eggs, room temperature
1 cup maple syrup
½ cup light brown sugar
1 teaspoon vanilla extract
¼ cup butter, melted
½ teaspoon ground cinnamon

Directions
1. Preheat the oven at 375°F (185°C).
2. Remove the chilled crust dough from the refrigerator.
3. Roll out the crust into a thin circle slightly bigger than a 9-inch pie pan.
4. Place the circle in the pie pan, crimp the edge, and cut off the excess dough.
5. In a large mixing bowl, whisk the eggs with a wire whisk.
6. Stir in the maple syrup, light brown sugar, vanilla, melted butter, and ground cinnamon.
7. Stir in the pecans and mix everything together.
8. Pour the mixture into the prepared crust.
9. Bake in the oven for about 50 minutes until the crust is golden brown and the filling is set.
10. Let cool, slice, and serve.

Nutrition per serving
Calories 663, fat 50.4 g, carbs 51 g, sugar 35 g,
Protein 8.8 g, sodium 175 mg

Bourbon Pecan Pie

Serves 8 | Prep time 10 minutes | Cooking time 30 minutes

Ingredients
1 recipe sablée crust (page 13)
½ cup sugar
½ cup light corn syrup
3 tablespoons butter, melted
½ cup brown sugar
2 cups pecan halves
2 tablespoons bourbon
3 eggs, beaten

Directions
1. Preheat the oven to 375°F (185°C).
2. Remove the chilled crust dough from the refrigerator.
3. Roll out the crust into a thin circle slightly bigger than a 9-inch pie pan.
4. Place the circle in the pie pan, crimp the edge, and cut off the excess dough.
5. In a large bowl, mix together the white sugar, brown sugar, and butter together. Stir in the eggs, corn syrup, and bourbon, and fold in the pecan halves.
6. Pour the filling into the pie crust.
7. Bake the pie in the preheated oven for 10 minutes, then reduce the heat to 350°F (177°C).
8. Continue to bake the pie for 25 minutes until the pie has set.
9. Cool on a cooling rack.

Nutrition per serving
Calories 537, fat 32 g, carbs 62 g, sugar 50 g,
Protein 6 g, sodium 306 mg

Pumpkin Pie

Serves 8 | Prep time 20 minutes | Cooking time 50 minutes

Ingredients
1 recipe brisée crust (page 12)
1½ cups pumpkin puree
1 can sweetened condensed milk
2 large eggs, room temperature
½ cup sugar
1 tablespoon all-purpose flour
1 teaspoon vanilla extract
½ teaspoon ground cinnamon

Directions
1. Preheat the oven at 375°F (185°C).
2. Remove the chilled crust dough from the refrigerator.
3. Roll out the crust into a thin circle slightly bigger than a 9-inch pie pan.
4. Place the circle in the pie pan, crimp the edge, and cut off the excess dough.
5. In a large mixing bowl, mix the pumpkin puree, sweetened condensed milk, eggs, sugar, flour, vanilla, and ground cinnamon.
6. Pour the mixture into the prepared crust.
7. Bake in the oven for about 50 minutes until the crust is golden brown and the filling is set.
8. Let cool, slice, and serve.

Nutrition per serving
Calories 294, fat 9.8 g, carbs 46.1 g, sugar 35.3 g,
Protein 6 g, sodium 170 mg

Pumpkin Orange Pie

Serves 8 | Prep time 20 minutes | Cooking time 50 minutes

Ingredients
1 recipe brisée crust (page 12)
1½ cups pumpkin puree
1 (14-ounce) can evaporated milk
2 large eggs, room temperature
1 cup sugar
Juice and zest of 1 orange
2 tablespoons all-purpose flour
1 teaspoon vanilla extract
½ teaspoon ground cinnamon

Directions
1. Preheat the oven at 375°F (185°C).
2. Remove the chilled crust dough from the refrigerator.
3. Roll out the crust into a thin circle slightly bigger than a 9-inch pie pan.
4. Place the circle in the pie pan, crimp the edge, and cut off the excess dough.
5. In a large mixing bowl, mix the pumpkin puree, evaporated milk, eggs, sugar, orange juice and zest, flour, vanilla, and ground cinnamon.
6. Pour the mixture into the prepared crust.
7. Bake in the oven for about 50 minutes until the crust is golden brown and the filling is set.
8. Let cool, slice, and serve.

Nutrition per serving
Calories 256, fat 14.9 g, carbs 45.2 g, sugar 17.9 g,
Protein 12.8 g, sodium 111 mg

Pumpkin Brûlée Pie

Serves 8 | Prep time 20 minutes | Cooking time 50 minutes

Ingredients
1 recipe brisée crust (page 12)
1½ cups pumpkin puree
1 (14-ounce) can sweetened condensed milk
3 large eggs, room temperature
1 cup sugar
1 tablespoon all-purpose flour
1 teaspoon vanilla extract
½ teaspoon ground cinnamon
3 tablespoons sugar, for garnish

Directions
1. Preheat the oven at 375°F (185°C).
2. Remove the chilled crust dough from the refrigerator.
3. Roll out the crust into a thin circle slightly bigger than a 9-inch pie pan.
4. Place the circle in the pie pan, crimp the edge, and cut off the excess dough.
5. In a large mixing bowl, mix the pumpkin puree, sweetened condensed milk, eggs, sugar, flour, vanilla, and ground cinnamon.
6. Pour the mixture into the prepared crust.
7. Bake in the oven for about 50 minutes until the crust is golden brown and the filling is set.
8. Let cool completely, top with sugar, and burn the sugar with a torch.
9. Slice and serve.

Nutrition per serving
Calories 356, fat 20.9 g, carbs 63.6 g, sugar 17.9 g,
Protein 12.5 g, sodium 125 mg

Sweet Potato Pie

Serves 8 | Prep time 20 minutes | Cooking time 50 minutes

Ingredients
1 recipe brisée crust (page 12)
2 pounds sweet potatoes, boiled and pureed
¼ cup butter
1 cup sugar
3 large eggs, room temperature
½ cup sweetened condensed milk
1¼ teaspoons ground cinnamon
¾ teaspoon ground ginger
¼ teaspoon ground cloves
1 teaspoon vanilla extract
1 cup heavy whipping cream
2 tablespoons icing sugar

Directions
1. Preheat the oven at 375°F (185°C).
2. Remove the chilled crust dough from the refrigerator.
3. Roll out the crust into a thin circle slightly bigger than a 9-inch pie pan.
4. Place the circle in the pie pan, crimp the edge, and cut off the excess dough.
5. In a large mixing bowl, mix the sweet potato puree, butter, sugar, eggs, sweetened condensed milk, cinnamon, ginger, and cloves until combined.
6. Pour the mixture into the prepared crust.
7. Bake in the oven for about 50 minutes until the crust is golden brown and the filling is set.
8. While the pie is cooling, whip the heavy whipping cream with the powdered sugar and vanilla until stiff peaks form.
9. Slice and serve with the whipped cream.

Nutrition per serving
Calories 511, fat 20.2 g, carbs 77.9 g, sugar 38.9 g,
Protein 6.7 g, sodium 210 mg

Sweet Potato Sour Cream Pie

Serves 8 | Prep time 20 minutes | Cooking time 55 minutes

Ingredients
1 recipe brisée crust (page 12)
1 pound sweet potatoes, boiled and mashed
1 cup sour cream
1 cup light brown sugar
3 large eggs, room temperature
1 teaspoon vanilla extract
1 tablespoon all-purpose flour
1 teaspoon ground cinnamon
½ teaspoon ground ginger
½ teaspoon ground nutmeg
1 cup heavy whipping cream, for garnish
2 tablespoons powdered sugar

Directions
1. Preheat the oven at 375°F (185°C).
2. Remove the chilled crust dough from the refrigerator.
3. Roll out the crust into a thin circle slightly bigger than a 9-inch pie pan.
4. Place the circle in the pie pan, crimp the edge, and cut off the excess dough.
5. In a large mixing bowl, mix the mashed sweet potatoes, sour cream, light brown sugar, eggs, vanilla, flour, cinnamon, ginger, and nutmeg.
6. Pour the mixture into the prepared crust.
7. Bake in the oven for about 50 minutes until the crust is golden brown and the filling is set. Let cool.
8. Whip the heavy whipping cream with the powdered sugar until stiff peaks form.
9. Slice and serve with the whipped cream.

Nutrition per serving
Calories 335, fat 22.3 g, carbs 29.9 g, sugar 17.9 g,
Protein 2.8 g, sodium 15 mg

Italian Ricotta Easter Pie

Serves 6–8 | Prep time 25 min. plus chilling time | Cooking time 55 min.

Ingredients
For the crust
1⅔ cups all-purpose flour
2 tablespoons sugar
¼ teaspoon salt
¼ teaspoon baking powder
½ cup butter
2 large eggs, lightly beaten
Icing sugar for dusting

For the filling
2 cups ricotta cheese
1 cup sugar
1 tablespoon cornstarch
½ teaspoon grated lemon zest
½ teaspoon grated orange zest
¼ teaspoon salt
4 large eggs
2 teaspoons vanilla extract
⅓ cup semisweet chocolate chips
⅓ cup diced citron, optional
Pinch ground cinnamon
Pinch ground nutmeg

Directions
1. In a mixing bowl, combine the flour, sugar, salt, and baking powder. Mix well.
2. Cut in the butter until a coarse meal is formed. Add the eggs and mix until the pastry comes together. Wrap and refrigerate for one hour.
3. Roll out the dough for a 9-inch pie plate. Trim and flute the edges. Refrigerate until ready to use.
4. Preheat the oven to 350°F (177°C).
5. To make the filling, beat the ricotta with sugar and cornstarch. Mix in the lemon and orange zest and the salt.

6. In a separate bowl, beat the eggs until they are thick and pale yellow, about 5 minutes. Gently fold them into the ricotta mixture together with the remaining ingredients.
7. Pour the filling into the crust and bake for 55 minutes, or until a knife inserted in the center comes out clean.
8. Let cool and refrigerate for 1 hour prior to serving. Dust pie with icing sugar before serving.

Nutrition per serving
Calories 299, fat 8 g, carbs 44 g, sugar 30 g,
Protein 12 g, sodium 224 mg

Spiced Plum Pie

Serves 8 | Prep time 20 minutes | Cooking time 55 minutes

Ingredients
1 recipe sucrée crust (page 11)
1 pound plums, sliced
2 teaspoons ground cinnamon
1 teaspoon ground nutmeg
½ teaspoon ground ginger
½ teaspoon ground allspice
2 tablespoons sugar
Juice of ½ lemon
2 tablespoons cornstarch
1 medium egg, slightly beaten

Directions
1. Preheat the oven at 375°F (185°C).
2. Remove the 2 chilled crust doughs from the refrigerator.
3. Roll out each dough into a thin circle slightly bigger than the pie pan.
4. Place one of the circles in the pie pan, crimp the edge, and cut off the excess dough.
5. In a large mixing bowl, mix the sliced plums, ground cinnamon, nutmeg, ginger, all-spice, sugar, lemon juice, and flour.
6. Transfer the plum filling into the pie crust and smooth it out with a spatula.
7. Cover with the other pie crust and seal the edges of the pie with a fork.
8. Brush the surface of the pie with a lightly whisked egg. Use a knife to make incisions so that the steam can escape while the pie bakes.
9. Bake in the oven for 50–55 minutes until the crust is golden brown.
10. Let cool, then slice and serve.

Nutrition per serving
Calories 107, fat 5.3 g, carbs 14.4 g, sugar 4.6 g,
Protein 0.8 g, sodium 103 mg

Holiday Chocolate Mint Pie

Serves 8 | Prep time | Cooking time 5 minutes
Chill time 4 hours 30 minutes

Ingredients
1 recipe Classic Amish pie crust, pre-baked (page 15)
1¼ cups milk
1 package chocolate pudding and pie filling mix
1 cup semisweet chocolate chips
½ cup milk
20 large marshmallows
1 cup whipping cream
½ teaspoon peppermint extract
6 tablespoons crushed hard peppermint candies

Directions
1. Preheat the oven to 350°F (177°C) and place the oven rack in the middle position.
2. Roll out the chilled dough into an 11-inch circle and place it into a 9-inch pie dish.
3. Crimp the edge, and cut off the excess dough.
4. Poke a few holes at the bottom of the pie crust with a fork. Place in the oven and bake for 8-10 minutes until golden and cooked through.
5. Remove from heat and let cool completely.
6. In a large saucepan, mix together the milk and the pudding mix over medium heat. Reduce the heat and continue cooking, adding the chocolate chips.
7. In another saucepan, heat the ½ cup of milk and the marshmallows until the marshmallows are melted.
8. Chill for about 30 minutes until the mixture forms mounds when dropped from a spoon.
9. In a chilled bowl, mix the whipping cream and the peppermint extract until stiff. Blend in the marshmallow mixture and the crushed candies.
10. Spoon the chocolate mixture into the cooled pie crust and top with the whipped cream mixture.
11. Place in the refrigerator for about 4 hours. Just before cutting, sprinkle with more crushed candies.

Nutrition per serving
Calories 431, fat 27 g, carbs 44 g, sugar 31 g,
Protein 3 g, sodium 302 mg

Ambrosia Pie

Serves 8 | Prep time 15 minutes | Cooking time 15 minutes

Ingredients
1 recipe Classic Amish pie crust, pre-baked (page 15)
2½ tablespoons cornstarch
¾ cup sugar
1 pinch of salt
¼ cup cold water
¾ cup boiling water
1 teaspoon grated orange rind
Juice and pulp of 1 large orange
3 eggs, separated
1 teaspoon lemon juice
½ cup flaked coconut
¼ teaspoon cream of tartar
¼ cup plus 2 tablespoons sugar

Directions
1. Preheat the oven to 350ºF (177ºC) and place the oven rack in the middle position.
2. Roll out the chilled dough into an 11-inch circle and place it into a 9-inch pie dish.
3. Crimp the edge, and cut off the excess dough.
4. Poke a few holes at the bottom of the pie crust with a fork. Place in the oven and bake for 8-10 minutes until golden and cooked through.
5. Remove from heat and let cool completely.
6. Combine the cornstarch, sugar, and salt.
7. Add the cold water, stirring until smooth.
8. Add the boiling water, mixing well. Stir in the orange rind, the juice, and the pulp.

9.   Beat the egg yolks and add them to the orange mixture.
10.   Cook over medium heat, stirring constantly, until smooth and thickened. Remove from the heat and stir in the lemon juice and the coconut.
11.   Pour this mixture into the pie crust.
12.   Beat the egg whites and the cream of tartar until it becomes foamy. Gradually add in the sugar, beating until it forms stiff peaks.
13.   Spread the meringue over the filling. Bake in the oven for about 15 minutes.

Nutrition per serving
Calories 246, fat 14 g, carbs 29 g, sugar 14 g,
Protein 1 g, sodium 190 mg

FUN FLAVORS

Chocolate Hazelnut Pie

Serves 8 | Prep time 20 minutes | Cooking time 50 minutes

Ingredients
1 recipe sablée crust (page 13)
⅓ cup light brown sugar
¾ cup chocolate hazelnut spread, melted or room temperature
5 ounces dark bittersweet chocolate, melted
3 large eggs, room temperature
1 (5-ounce) can sweetened condensed milk
¼ cup butter, melted
5 ounces raspberries, fresh or frozen

Directions
1. Preheat the oven at 375°F (185°C).
2. Remove the chilled crust dough from the refrigerator.
3. Roll out the crust into a thin circle slightly bigger than a 9-inch pie pan.
4. Place the circle in the pie pan, crimp the edge, and cut off the excess dough.
5. In a large mixing bowl, mix the eggs with the light brown sugar, melted chocolate, chocolate hazelnut spread, sweetened condensed milk, and melted butter.
6. Pour the mixture into the prepared crust.
7. Bake in the oven for about 50 minutes until the crust is golden brown and the filling is set.
8. Let cool, dust with powdered sugar, slice, and serve.

Nutrition per serving
Calories 452, fat 20.5 g, carbs 85.6 g, sugar 35.6 g,
Protein 15.6 g, sodium 115 mg

Chocolate Pecan Coconut Pie

Serves 16 | Prep time 15 minutes | Cooking time 45 minutes

Ingredients
1 recipe American flaky pie crust (page 9)
7 tablespoons baking cocoa
3 cups sugar
½ cup butter
4 eggs, beaten
13 ounces evaporated milk
1 teaspoon vanilla
1 cup chopped pecans
2 cups flaked coconut

Directions
1. Preheat the oven to 350°F (177°C).
2. Remove the 2 chilled crust doughs from the refrigerator.
3. Roll out each dough into a thin circle slightly bigger than the pie pan.
4. Place one circle on one pie pan each, crimp the edges, and cut off the excess dough.
5. Melt the margarine and set it aside. In a bowl, mix together the sugar and the cocoa.
6. Mix in the milk, the butter, the eggs, and the vanilla.
7. Stir in the coconut and the pecans and pour into the 2 pie crusts.
8. Bake in the oven for 45 minutes. Cool on racks.

Nutrition per serving
Calories 756, fat 21 g, carbs 84 g, sugar 59 g,
Protein 8 g, sodium 386 mg

Chocolate Mint Custard Pie

Serves 8 | Prep time 15 minutes | Cooking time 10 minutes
Chill time 4 hours

Ingredients
2 cups chocolate cookie crumbs
¼ cup margarine or unsalted butter, melted
1 tablespoon honey
½ cup sugar, or preferred sugar substitute
3 tablespoons corn starch
2 cups low fat milk
¼ cup fresh mint, chopped
4 egg yolks
1 teaspoon vanilla extract
2 tablespoons margarine
2 tablespoons dark cocoa powder
½ cup dark chocolate pieces, chopped

Directions
1. Preheat the oven to 350°F (177°C).
2. Combine the cookie crumbs, melted margarine, and honey. Mix well and press into a pie dish.
3. Place in the oven and bake for 10-15 minutes. Remove from the oven and allow to cool completely.
4. Heat one cup of the milk, along with the vanilla extract and mint in a saucepan over low heat, until steamy.
5. In a bowl, combine the sugar, cornstarch, and remaining milk. Mix well. Add the egg yolks and mix until completely combined.
6. Slowly pour the warmed milk into the mixture, whisking constantly to prevent the egg yolks from scrambling.
7. Once the yolks are tempered, pour the entire mixture into the saucepan and cook over medium heat, until a gentle boil forms and the custard thickens.
8. Stir in the margarine, cocoa powder, and dark chocolate pieces.
9. Stir until melted and completely blended.
10. Pour the custard into the pie dish.
11. Place in the refrigerator and chill for at least 4 hours, or until completely set, before slicing.

Nutrition per serving
Calories 286.5, carbohydrates 38.6 g, fat 13.1 g,
Sugars 24.3 g, sodium 261.1 mg

Nutrition per serving
Calories 448, fat 28 g, carbs 47 g, sugar 32 g,
Protein 2 g, sodium 410 mg

Easy Chocolate Mint Pie

Serves 8 | Prep time 20 minutes | Cooking time 50 minutes

Ingredients
1 recipe sablée crust (page 13)
⅓ cup sugar
⅓ cup cocoa powder
1 teaspoon peppermint extract
2 large eggs, room temperature
1 (5-ounce) can sweetened condensed milk
¼ cup butter, melted

Directions
1. Preheat the oven at 375°F (185°C).
2. Remove the chilled crust dough from the refrigerator.
3. Roll out the crust into a thin circle slightly bigger than a 9-inch pie pan.
4. Place the circle in the pie pan, crimp the edge, and cut off the excess dough.
5. In a large mixing bowl, mix the eggs with the sugar, peppermint extract, cocoa powder, sweetened condensed milk, and melted butter.
6. Pour the mixture into the prepared crust.
7. Bake in the oven for about 50 minutes until the crust is golden brown and the filling is set.
8. Let cool, dust with powdered sugar, slice, and serve.

Nutrition per serving
Calories 386, fat 25.3 g, carbs 82.6 g, sugar 42.3 g,
Protein 15.6 g, sodium 189 mg

Brownie Pie

Serves 8 | Prep time 15 minutes | Cooking time 35 minutes

Ingredients
1 recipe sablée crust (page 13)
1 (23-ounce) box brownie mix
½ cup water
1 large egg
1 teaspoon vanilla extract

Directions
1. Preheat the oven at 375°F (185°C).
2. Remove the chilled crust dough from the refrigerator.
3. Roll out the crust into a thin circle slightly bigger than a 9-inch pie pan.
4. Place the circle in the pie pan, crimp the edge, and cut off the excess dough.
5. In a large mixing bowl, mix the brownie mix with the water, egg, and vanilla.
6. Pour the mixture into the prepared crust.
7. Bake in the oven for about 35 minutes until the crust is golden brown and the filling is set.
8. Let cool, slice, and serve.

Nutrition per serving
Calories 356, fat 56 g, carbs 56.2 g, sugar 19.5 g,
Protein 14.2 g, sodium 457 mg

Black Bottom Hazelnut Pie

Serves 8 | Prep time 20 minutes | Cooking time 50 minutes

Ingredients
1 recipe sablée crust (page 13)
3 cups blanched hazelnuts
4 ounces dark chocolate, chopped
6 tablespoons butter
1 cup light brown sugar
1 tablespoon instant espresso powder
1 tablespoon vanilla extract
1 cup light corn syrup
3 large eggs, room temperature

Directions
1. Preheat the oven at 375°F (185°C).
2. Remove the chilled crust dough from the refrigerator.
3. Roll out the crust into a thin circle slightly bigger than a 9-inch pie pan.
4. Place the circle in the pie pan, crimp the edge, and cut off the excess dough.
5. In a large mixing bowl, mix the light brown sugar with the corn syrup, eggs, vanilla, espresso powder, melted butter, chopped chocolate, and blanched hazelnuts.
6. Pour the mixture into the prepared crust.
7. Bake in the oven for about 50 minutes until the crust is golden brown and the filling is set.
8. Let cool, dust with powdered sugar, slice, and serve.

Nutrition per serving
Calories 356, fat 20.6 g, carbs 189 g, sugar 46.5 g,
Protein 12.8 g, sodium 456 mg

Dulce de Leche Pumpkin Pie

Serves 8 | Prep time 20 minutes | Cooking time 55 minutes

Ingredients
1 recipe brisée crust (page 12)
1½ cups pumpkin puree
1 (14-ounce) can dulce de leche
2 large eggs, room temperature
1 tablespoon all-purpose flour
1 teaspoon vanilla extract
½ teaspoon ground cinnamon

Directions
1. Preheat the oven at 375°F (185°C).
2. Remove the chilled crust dough from the refrigerator.
3. Roll out the crust into a thin circle slightly bigger than a 9-inch pie pan.
4. Place the circle in the pie pan, crimp the edge, and cut off the excess dough.
5. In a large mixing bowl, mix the pumpkin puree, dulce de leche, eggs, flour, vanilla, and ground cinnamon.
6. Pour the mixture into the prepared crust.
7. Bake in the oven for about 50 minutes until the crust is golden brown and the filling is set.
8. Let cool, slice, and serve.

Nutrition per serving
Calories 335, fat 15.4 g, carbs 47.4 g, sugar 33 g,
Protein 3.4 g, sodium 207 mg

Salted Caramel Peanut Butter Fudge Pie

Serves 8 | Prep time 20 minutes | Cooking time 50 minutes

Ingredients
1 recipe brisée crust (page 12)
¾ cup butter
½ cup creamy peanut butter
1 cup light brown sugar
1 cup all-purpose flour
½ cup roasted peanuts
3 ounces dark chocolate
½ cup sugar
2 tablespoons cocoa powder
3 large eggs, room temperature
2 teaspoons vanilla extract
Caramel sauce, for drizzling

Directions
1. Preheat the oven at 375°F (185°C).
2. Remove the chilled crust dough from the refrigerator.
3. Roll out the crust into a thin circle slightly bigger than a 9-inch pie pan.
4. Place the circle in the pie pan, crimp the edge, and cut off the excess dough.
5. In a microwave-safe bowl, melt the butter with the dark chocolate.
6. Stir in the peanut butter and mix until everything is combined. Stir in the light brown sugar, roasted peanuts, sugar, and eggs, and mix until combined.
7. Stir in the vanilla, cocoa powder, and flour. Mix until everything is combined.
8. Pour the mixture into the prepared crust.
9. Bake in the oven for about 50 minutes until the crust is golden brown and the filling is set.
10. Let cool, drizzle with caramel sauce, slice, and serve.

Nutrition per serving
Calories 761, fat 42.7 g, carbs 87.2 g, sugar 49.2 g,
Protein 13.2 g, sodium 481 mg

Macadamia Pie

Serves 8 | Prep time 20 minutes | Cooking time 55 minutes

Ingredients
1 recipe brisée crust (page 12)
3 large eggs, room temperature
1¼ cups light brown sugar
1 teaspoon vanilla extract
½ cup butter, melted
1½ cups dry roasted macadamia nuts, roughly chopped
1 cup toasted coconut flakes

Directions
1. Preheat the oven at 375°F (185°C).
2. Remove the chilled crust dough from the refrigerator.
3. Roll out the crust into a thin circle slightly bigger than a 9-inch pie pan.
4. Place the circle in the pie pan, crimp the edge, and cut off the excess dough.
5. In a large mixing bowl, mix the eggs with light brown sugar, vanilla, and melted butter.
6. Stir in the roasted macadamia nuts and toasted coconut flakes.
7. Pour the mixture into the prepared crust.
8. Bake in the oven for about 50 minutes until the crust is golden brown and the filling is set.
9. Let cool, slice, and serve.

Nutrition per serving
Calories 452, fat 25.6 g, carbs 56 g, sugar 25.6 g,
Protein 15.2 g, sodium 53 mg

Burnt Caramel Pie

Serves 10 | Prep time 30 min. | Chilling time 1 hour
Cooking time 30 min.

Ingredients

For the crust
2⅔ cups all-purpose flour
2 tablespoons sugar
½ teaspoon salt
½ cup cold, unsalted butter, cubed
6 tablespoons cold vegetable shortening
2 teaspoons vinegar
½ cup ice water

For the filling
4 eggs, separated
1 cup evaporated milk
½ cup light corn syrup
¼ cup butter, melted
½ teaspoon vanilla extract
3 cups white sugar, divided
½ cup all-purpose flour
3 cups water
½ teaspoon cream of tartar

Directions

1. Prepare the crusts. In a large bowl, combine the flour, sugar, and salt.
2. Cut in the butter and vegetable shortening with a pastry cutter or two knives until the mixture has pea-sized crumbs.
3. Gradually mix in the water just until the dough comes together. Be careful not to overwork the dough. Divide it in half and shape both into disks. Wrap in plastic and refrigerate for at least an hour.
4. Preheat the oven to 375°F (190°C) and set out two 9-inch pie plates.
5. Roll the dough into two 9-inch circles and arrange one on each pie plate. Trim and flute the edges. Place a piece of foil in each pie crust and fill them with dry beans or pie weights.

6. Bake for 15 minutes and then remove the foil and weights. Continue to bake the crusts for 10 more minutes, or until golden. Set them aside to cool.
7. Combine the egg yolks, evaporated milk, syrup, melted butter, vanilla, half a cup of sugar, and flour.
8. Heat the oven to 325°F (163°C).
9. Heat a cast-iron skillet and brown 2 cups of the sugar until golden.
10. Remove the pan from the heat and stir in the water. Stir until the sugar dissolves, returning the skillet to the heat.
11. Whisk in the egg yolk mixture and cook until it thickens, and then five minutes more. Pour the filling into the prepared pie crust.
12. Beat the egg whites until foamy. Add the cream of tartar and gradually beat in the remaining half cup of sugar.
13. Beat until stiff peaks form, and spread the meringue over the pies.
14. Bake for 15 minutes, until the meringue is golden.

Nutrition per serving
Calories 481, fat 14 g, carbs 61 g, sugar 42 g,
Protein 4 g, sodium 193 mg

Coconut Macaroon Pie

Serves 8 | Prep time 20 minutes | Cooking time 55 minutes

Ingredients
1 recipe brisée crust (page 12)
2 large eggs, room temperature
1 (14-ounce) can sweetened condensed milk
¼ cup butter, melted
1 teaspoon vanilla extract
¼ cup flour
1 (14-ounce) package sweetened shredded coconut flakes

Directions
1. Preheat the oven at 375°F (185°C).
2. Remove the chilled crust dough from the refrigerator.
3. Roll out the crust into a thin circle slightly bigger than a 9-inch pie pan.
4. Place the circle in the pie pan, crimp the edge, and cut off the excess dough.
5. In a large mixing bowl, mix the eggs with the sweetened condensed milk, melted butter, vanilla, and flour.
6. Reserve ½ cup of the coconut flakes and stir the remainder into the filling.
7. Pour the mixture into the prepared crust.
8. Bake in the oven for about 50 minutes until the crust is golden brown and the filling is set.
9. Meanwhile, toast the remaining coconut flakes.
10. Let cool, sprinkle with toasted coconut flakes, slice, and serve.

Nutrition per serving
Calories 389, fat 23.5 g, carbs 26.5 g, sugar 45.8 g,
Protein 20.6 g, sodium 24.6 mg

Maple Walnut Pie

Serves 8 | Prep time 20 minutes | Cooking time 50 minutes

Ingredients
1 recipe brisée crust (page 12)
2½ cups toasted walnuts
3 large eggs, room temperature
1 cup maple syrup
½ cup light brown sugar
1 teaspoon vanilla extract
¼ cup butter, melted
2 tablespoons all-purpose flour
½ teaspoon ground cinnamon

Directions
1. Preheat the oven at 375°F (185°C).
2. Remove the chilled crust dough from the refrigerator.
3. Roll out the crust into a thin circle slightly bigger than a 9-inch pie pan.
4. Place the circle in the pie pan, crimp the edge, and cut off the excess dough.
5. In a large mixing bowl, whisk the eggs.
6. Stir in the maple syrup, light brown sugar, vanilla, melted butter, flour, and ground cinnamon.
7. Stir in the toasted walnuts and mix everything together.
8. Pour the mixture into the prepared crust.
9. Bake in the oven for about 50 minutes until the crust is golden brown and the filling is set.
10. Let cool, slice, and serve.

Nutrition per serving
Calories 523, fat 125g, carbs 125 g, sugar 60.2 g,
Protein 20.3 g, sodium 145 mg

Honey Pistachio Pie

Serves 8 | Prep time 20 minutes | Cooking time 50 minutes

Ingredients
1 recipe brisée crust (page 12)
2½ cups toasted pistachios
3 large eggs, room temperature
1 cup honey
½ cup sugar
1 teaspoon vanilla extract
¼ cup butter, melted
2 tablespoons all-purpose flour
½ teaspoon ground cardamom

Directions
1. Preheat the oven at 375°F (185°C).
2. Remove the chilled crust dough from the refrigerator.
3. Roll out the crust into a thin circle slightly bigger than a 9-inch pie pan.
4. Place the circle in the pie pan, crimp the edge, and cut off the excess dough.
5. In a large mixing bowl, whisk the eggs with a wire whisk.
6. Stir in the honey, sugar, vanilla, melted butter, flour, and ground cardamom.
7. Stir in the toasted pistachios and mix everything together.
8. Pour the mixture into the prepared crust.
9. Bake in the oven for about 50 minutes until the crust is golden brown and the filling is set.
10. Let cool, slice, and serve.

Nutrition per serving
Calories 510, fat 23.8 g, carbs 73.7 g, sugar 60.2 g,
Protein 7.8 g, sodium 340 mg

Walnut and Carrot Pie

Serves 8 | Prep time 20 minutes | Cooking time 50 minutes

Ingredients
1 recipe brisée crust (page 12)
2 cups toasted walnuts
3 medium carrots, grated
3 large eggs, room temperature
1 cup corn syrup
½ cup light brown sugar
1 teaspoon vanilla extract
¼ cup butter, melted
2 tablespoons all-purpose flour
½ teaspoon ground cinnamon

Directions
1. Preheat the oven at 375°F (185°C).
2. Remove the chilled crust dough from the refrigerator.
3. Roll out the crust into a thin circle slightly bigger than a 9-inch pie pan.
4. Place the circle in the pie pan, crimp the edge, and cut off the excess dough.
5. In a large mixing bowl, whisk the eggs with a wire whisk.
6. Stir in the corn syrup, light brown sugar, vanilla, melted butter, flour, and ground cinnamon.
7. Stir in the toasted walnuts and shredded carrots and mix everything together.
8. Pour the mixture into the prepared crust.
9. Bake in the oven for about 50 minutes until the crust is golden brown and the filling is set.
10. Let cool, slice, and serve.

Nutrition per serving
Calories 514, fat 31.3 g, carbs 53.3 g, sugar 21.4 g,
Protein 11 g, sodium 189 mg

Oat and Honey Granola Pie

Serves 8 | Prep time 20 minutes | Cooking time 50 minutes

Ingredients
1 recipe brisée crust (page 12)
½ cup butter, melted
¾ cup maple syrup
1 teaspoon vanilla extract
3 large eggs, room temperature
1 cup nutty granola
¼ cup old-fashioned oats
¼ cup chocolate chips
½ cup walnuts, roughly chopped

Directions
1. Preheat the oven at 375°F (185°C).
2. Remove the chilled crust dough from the refrigerator.
3. Roll out the crust into a thin circle slightly bigger than a 9-inch pie pan.
4. Place the circle in the pie pan, crimp the edge, and cut off the excess dough.
5. In a large mixing bowl, mix the melted butter, maple syrup, vanilla, eggs, granola, oats, chocolate chips, and walnuts.
6. Pour the mixture into the prepared crust.
7. Bake in the oven for about 50 minutes until the crust is golden brown and the filling is set.
8. Let cool, then slice and serve.

Nutrition per serving
Calories 411, fat 26 g, carbs 39 g, sugar 23.5 g,
Protein 7.5 g, sodium 274 mg

Cheesecake Pie

Serves 8 | Prep time 20 minutes | Cooking time 50 minutes

Ingredients
1 recipe brisée crust (page 12)
1 pound cream cheese, softened
2 large eggs, room temperature
⅔ cup sugar
1 teaspoon vanilla extract
Chocolate shavings for serving

Directions
1. Preheat the oven at 375°F (185°C).
2. Remove the chilled crust dough from the refrigerator.
3. Roll out the crust into a thin circle slightly bigger than a 9-inch pie pan.
4. Place the circle in the pie pan, crimp the edge, and cut off the excess dough.
5. In a large mixing bowl, mix the cream cheese, eggs, sugar, and vanilla.
6. Pour the mixture into the prepared crust.
7. Bake in the oven for about 50 minutes until the crust is golden brown and the filling is set.
8. Let cool, decorate with chocolate shavings if desired. Slice and serve.

Nutrition per serving
Calories 427, fat 28.5 g, carbs 37.8 g, sugar 28.4 g,
Protein 7.1 g, sodium 356 mg

Oatmeal Vanilla Pie

Serves: 8 | Prep time 5–10 minutes
Cooking time 40–45 minutes

Ingredients
1 recipe brisée crust (page 12)
1 cup molasses
4 eggs, beaten
¾ cup milk
1 cup sugar
1 tablespoon butter, melted
1½ cups quick-cooking oatmeal
2 teaspoons vanilla extract
½ cup chopped walnuts
¼ teaspoon salt

Directions
1. Preheat an oven to 350°F (177°C).
2. Remove the chilled crust dough from the refrigerator.
3. Roll out the crust into a thin circle slightly bigger than a 9-inch pie pan.
4. Place the circle in the pie pan, crimp the edge, and cut off the excess dough.
5. In a large bowl, add in the above-mentioned ingredients one by one; thoroughly mix them all using a kitchen spatula.
6. Pour the mixture into the crust.
7. Bake for 40–45 minutes.
8. Take out, cool down for a few minutes, and serve warm (or refrigerate for a few hours).

Nutrition per serving
Calories 391, carbs 69g, fat 10.5g,
Protein 7.5g, sodium 159mg

NO-BAKE PIES

Cookies and Cream Pie

Serves 8 | Prep time 20 minutes | Chill time 4 hours

Ingredients
1 recipe graham cracker crust (page 14)
2 cups heavy whipping cream
2 tablespoons powdered sugar
1 teaspoon vanilla extract
15 Oreos, crushed
1 package instant chocolate pudding
1½ cups half and half
Chocolate shavings for garnish

Directions
1. Remove the chilled crust dough from the refrigerator.
2. In a bowl, whisk together the chocolate pudding and the half and half. Let set until firm.
3. Whip the heavy whipping cream with powdered sugar and vanilla. Fold in the chocolate pudding.
4. Stir in the crushed Oreos. Pour the filling into the pie crust and smooth with a spatula.
5. Chill in the refrigerator for 4 hours before serving.
6. Just before serving, sprinkle with chocolate shavings.

Nutrition per serving
Calories 421, fat 27.3 g, carbs 40.9 g, sugar 23.7 g,
Protein 4.2 g, sodium 346 mg

Butterfinger Pie

Serves 8 | Prep time 20 minutes | Chill time 4 hours

Ingredients
1 recipe graham cracker crust (page 14)
8 ounces cream cheese, softened
½ cup creamy peanut butter
1 teaspoon vanilla extract
1½ cups powdered sugar
2½ cups Butterfinger candy bars, roughly chopped
8 ounces whipped cream

Directions
1. Remove the chilled crust dough from the refrigerator.
2. In the bowl of a stand mixer, whip the cream cheese with the peanut butter, vanilla, and powdered sugar until creamy.
3. Stir in the chopped Butterfinger candy bars and fold in the whipped cream.
4. Pour the prepared mixture into the chilled crust dough and smooth it out with a spatula.
5. Sprinkle with more chopped Butterfingers on top, if desired.
6. Chill for about 4 hours before serving.
7. Cut into 8 slices and serve.

Nutrition per serving
Calories 707, fat 35.8 g, carbs 91.2 g, sugar 65.7 g,
Protein 10.3 g, sodium 453 mg

Lemon Pie

Serves 8 | Prep time 20 minutes | Chill time 4 hours

Ingredients
1 recipe graham cracker crust (page 14)
1 pound cream cheese, softened
1 teaspoon vanilla extract
1½ cups powdered sugar
Zest of 1 lemon
Juice of 2 lemons
1 cup whipping cream

Directions
1. Remove the chilled crust dough from the refrigerator.
2. In the bowl of a stand mixer, whip the cream cheese with the vanilla and powdered sugar until creamy.
3. Stir in the lemon juice and zest and fold everything together.
4. In a separate bowl, whip the whipping cream until stiff peaks form. Fold it into the cream cheese mixture.
5. Pour the prepared mixture into the chilled crust and smooth it out with a spatula.
6. Chill for about 4 hours before serving.
7. Cut into 8 slices and garnish with lemon slices.

Nutrition per serving
Calories 480, fat 31.9 g, carbs 44.5 g, sugar 34.4 g,
Protein 5.9 g, sodium 344 mg

Strawberry and Mascarpone Pie

Serves 8 | Prep time 20 minutes | Chill time 4 hours

Ingredients
1 recipe graham cracker crust (page 14)
8 ounces cream cheese, softened
1 teaspoon vanilla extract
1 cup powdered sugar
Juice of ½ lemon
5 ounces mascarpone cheese, softened
1 cup whipping cream, chilled
10 ounces fresh strawberries, diced, for garnish

Directions
1. Remove the chilled crust dough from the refrigerator.
2. In the bowl of a stand mixer, whip the cream cheese with vanilla, mascarpone cheese, and powdered sugar until creamy.
3. Stir in the lemon juice and fold everything together.
4. In a separate bowl, whip the whipping cream until stiff peaks form. Fold it into the cream cheese mixture.
5. Pour the prepared mixture into the chilled crust and smooth it out with a spatula.
6. Chill for about 4 hours before serving.
7. Cut into 8 slices and garnish with diced strawberries.

Nutrition per serving
Calories 259, fat 17.8 g, carbs 21 g, sugar 17.4 g,
Protein 4.8 g, sodium 111 mg

Chocolate S'mores Pie

Serves 8 | Prep time 20 minutes | Chill time 4 hours

Ingredients
1 recipe graham cracker crust (page 14)
2 cups heavy whipping cream
2 tablespoons powdered sugar
1 teaspoon vanilla extract
1 package instant chocolate pudding
1½ cups whole milk
1 bag of marshmallows, for decoration

Directions
1. Remove the chilled crust dough from the refrigerator.
2. In a bowl, whisk together the instant chocolate pudding and whole milk. Let set until firm.
3. Whip the heavy whipping cream with powdered sugar and vanilla. Fold in the chocolate pudding.
4. Pour the filling into the pie crust and smooth with a spatula.
5. Chill in the refrigerator for 4 hours before serving.
6. Just before serving, top the pie with marshmallows and burn them with a torch so they melt. Alternatively, you can use marshmallow fluff for this step.

Nutrition per serving
Calories 256, fat 13.6 g, carbs 31 g, sugar 17.5 g,
Protein 2.5 g, sodium 226 mg

Pistachio Cream Pie

Serves 8 | Prep time 20 minutes | Chill time 4 hours

Ingredients
1 recipe graham cracker crust (page 14)
8 ounces cream cheese, softened
1 cup whole milk
1 teaspoon vanilla extract
1 package instant pistachio pudding mix
2 cups heavy whipping cream
3 tablespoons icing sugar
1 (8-ounce) can crushed pineapple
3–4 tablespoons pistachios, chopped, for decoration

Directions
1. Remove the chilled crust dough from the refrigerator.
2. In the bowl of a stand mixer, whip the cream cheese with the vanilla, instant pistachio pudding mix, and whole milk until creamy.
3. Stir in the crushed pineapple and fold everything together.
4. Pour the prepared mixture into the chilled crust and smooth it out with a spatula.
5. Chill in the refrigerator for about 4 hours.
6. Mix the heavy whipping cream with the powdered sugar until medium-stiff peaks form. Dollop on top of the pie.
7. Sprinkle with chopped pistachios and serve.

Nutrition per serving
Calories 259, fat 23.5 g, carbs 8.7 g, sugar 5.6 g,
Protein 4.2 g, sodium 164 mg

Molasses Cream Pie

Serves 8 | Prep time 20 minutes | Chill time 4 hours

Ingredients
1 recipe graham cracker crust (page 14)
1½ pounds cream cheese, softened
½ cup light brown sugar
1 teaspoon vanilla extract
¼ cup molasses
1½ teaspoon ground cinnamon
½ teaspoon ground ginger
¼ teaspoon allspice
8 ounces Cool Whip
Caramel sauce for serving

Directions
1. Remove the chilled crust dough from the refrigerator.
2. In the bowl of a stand mixer, whip the cream cheese with vanilla, light brown sugar, and molasses until creamy.
3. Stir in the ground cinnamon, ground ginger, allspice, and Cool Whip and fold everything together.
4. Pour the prepared mixture into the chilled crust and smooth it out with a spatula.
5. Chill in the refrigerator for about 4 hours.
6. Just before serving, cut the pie and drizzle some caramel sauce on top of every piece.

Nutrition per serving
Calories 481, fat 37.8 g, carbs 30.8 g, sugar 22 g,
Protein 7 g, sodium 290 mg

Snickers Pie

Serves 8 | Prep time 20 minutes | Chill time 4 hours

Ingredients
1 recipe graham cracker crust (page 14)
8 ounces cream cheese, softened
½ cup dulce de leche
1 teaspoon vanilla extract
1 cup powdered sugar
8 ounces Cool Whip
3 Snickers candy bars, chopped, for decoration
¼ cup peanuts, chopped
3 ounces chocolate, melted

Directions
1. Remove the chilled crust dough from the refrigerator.
2. In the bowl of a stand mixer, whip the cream cheese with the dulce de leche, vanilla, powdered sugar, and Cool Whip until creamy.
3. Pour the prepared mixture into the chilled crust and smooth it out with a spatula.
4. Sprinkle with some chopped peanuts and Snickers bars.
5. Chill for about 4 hours before serving.
6. Cut into 8 slices and serve.

Nutrition per serving
Calories 426, fat 25.6 g, carbs 45.3 g, sugar 39.9 g,
Protein 6 g, sodium 143 mg

Banana Cream Pie

Serves 8 | Prep time 20 minutes | Chill time 4 hours

Ingredients
1 recipe graham cracker crust (page 14)
1¾ cups whole milk
½ cup heavy whipping cream
2 packages instant banana pudding
1 teaspoon vanilla extract
4 bananas, cut into circles
Ground cinnamon for garnish

Directions
1. Remove the chilled crust dough from the refrigerator.
2. In a bowl, mix the whole milk with the instant banana pudding. Let it sit for a while.
3. Whip the heavy whipping cream until stiff peaks form. Fold in the pudding mixture and vanilla.
4. Arrange the banana slices in the crust.
5. Pour the prepared banana pudding mixture into the crust and smooth it out with a spatula.
6. Sprinkle with some ground cinnamon.
7. Chill for about 4 hours before serving.
8. Cut into 8 slices and serve.

Nutrition per serving
Calories 152, fat 6 g, carbs 22.6 g, sugar 10.9 g,
Protein 3.3 g, sodium 105 mg

Peanut Butter Pie

Serves 8 | Prep time 20 minutes | Chill time 4 hours

Ingredients
1 recipe graham cracker crust (page 14)
1 cup smooth peanut butter
3 ripe medium bananas, slightly mashed
8 ounces Cool Whip
2 teaspoons vanilla extract
½ cup chocolate chips

Directions
1. Remove the chilled crust dough from the refrigerator.
2. In the bowl of an electric mixer, mix the peanut butter, vanilla, and bananas until combined.
3. Stir the Cool Whip into the mixture.
4. Pour the mixture into the pie crust and chill in the refrigerator for about 4 hours.
5. Just before serving, sprinkle with chocolate chips.

Nutrition per serving
Calories 392, fat 27.6 g, carbs 30.9 g, sugar 21.3 g,
Protein 9.8 g, sodium 170 mg

Blueberry Cream Cheese Pie

Serves 8 | Prep time 20 minutes | Chill time 4 hours

Ingredients
1 recipe graham cracker crust (page 14)
12 ounces cream cheese, softened
2 tablespoons Greek yogurt
2 tablespoons lemon juice
¾ cup powdered sugar
½ cup heavy whipping cream
1 envelope gelatin, dissolved in water
10 ounces fresh blueberries

Directions
1. Remove the chilled crust dough from the refrigerator.
2. In the bowl of an electric mixer, beat the cream cheese, Greek yogurt, lemon juice, and powdered sugar.
3. In another bowl, whip the heavy whipping cream until stiff peaks form. Fold it into the cream cheese mixture.
4. Mix until combined, then stir in the dissolved gelatin and fresh blueberries.
5. Pour the mixture into the pie crust and chill in the refrigerator for about 4 hours.
6. Just before serving, sprinkle with fresh blueberries.

Nutrition per serving
Calories 258, fat 18.7 g, carbs 19.4 g, sugar 15.6 g,
Protein 4.8 g, sodium 139 mg

Peaches and Cream Pie

Serves 8 | Prep time 20 minutes | Chill time 4 hours

Ingredients
1 recipe graham cracker crust (page 14)
5 ounces cream cheese, softened
⅓ cup powdered sugar
1 teaspoon vanilla extract
8 ounces Cool Whip
3 peaches, sliced into wedges
3 tablespoons apricot jam, hot

Directions
1. Remove the chilled crust dough from the refrigerator.
2. In the bowl of an electric mixer, beat the cream cheese, vanilla, and powdered sugar.
3. Fold the Cool Whip into the mixture and mix everything together.
4. Pour the mixture into the pie crust and chill in the refrigerator for about 4 hours.
5. Just before serving, top with peach wedges and brush the whole surface with hot apricot jam.
6. Slice and serve.

Nutrition per serving
Calories 227, fat 14.4 g, carbs 23.6 g, sugar 20.8 g,
Protein 2.4 g, sodium 69 mg

White Chocolate Pie

Serves 8 | Prep time 20 minutes | Chill time 4 hours

Ingredients
1 recipe graham cracker crust (page 14)
8 ounces cream cheese, softened
8 ounces white chocolate, melted and cooled
½ cup powdered sugar
8 ounces Cool Whip
1 teaspoon vanilla extract
2 cups mixed fresh berries

Directions
1. Remove the chilled crust dough from the refrigerator.
2. In the bowl of an electric mixer, beat the cream cheese, white chocolate, vanilla, and powdered sugar.
3. Fold the Cool Whip into the mixture and mix everything together.
4. Pour the mixture into the pie crust and chill in the refrigerator for about 4 hours.
5. Just before serving, top with fresh berries.
6. Slice and serve.

Nutrition per serving
Calories 414, fat 27.1 g, carbs 39.6 g, sugar 37 g,
Protein 4.5 g, sodium 124 mg

Nutella Pie

Serves 8 | Prep time 15 minutes | Chill time 4 hours

Ingredients
1 recipe graham cracker crust (page 14)
1 pound cream cheese, softened
1 cup Nutella, room temperature
3 tablespoons powdered sugar
1 cup heavy whipping cream
1 teaspoon vanilla extract
¼ cup ground hazelnuts

Directions
1. Remove the chilled crust dough from the refrigerator.
2. In the bowl of an electric mixer, beat the cream cheese, Nutella, vanilla, and powdered sugar.
3. Whip the heavy cream into stiff peaks and fold it into the mixture.
4. Pour the mixture into the pie crust. Chill for about 4 hours in the refrigerator or 40 minutes in the freezer.
5. Just before serving, top with chopped hazelnuts.
6. Slice and serve.

Nutrition per serving
Calories 316, fat 29 g, carbs 9.8 g, sugar 6.5 g,
Protein 5.3 g, sodium 182 mg

Millionaire Pie

Serves 8 | Prep time 15 minutes | Chill time 4 hours

Ingredients
1 recipe graham cracker crust (page 14)
1 cup shredded coconut
1 (15-ounce) can crushed pineapple, drained
1 cup maraschino cherries, drained and chopped
½ cup pecans, chopped
1 (14-ounce) can sweetened condensed milk
5 tablespoons lemon juice
1½ cups Cool Whip

Directions
1. Remove the chilled crust dough from the refrigerator.
2. In a large mixing bowl, combine the shredded coconut, crushed pineapple, maraschino cherries, and pecans.
3. Stir in the condensed milk and lemon juice.
4. Carefully fold in the Cool Whip.
5. Pour the mixture into the pie crust and chill in the refrigerator for about 4 hours.
6. Just before serving, top with extra maraschino cherries, if desired.
7. Slice and serve.

Nutrition per serving
Calories 414, fat 23.7 g, carbs 47.8 g, sugar 41.6 g,
Protein 7.2 g, sodium 89 mg

Orange Pie

Serves 8 | Prep time 20 minutes | Chill time 4 hours

Ingredients
1 recipe graham cracker crust (page 14)
1 pound cream cheese, softened
1 teaspoon vanilla extract
1½ cups powdered sugar
Zest of 1 orange
Juice of 2 oranges
1 envelope gelatin, dissolved in water
1 cup whipping cream

Directions
1. Remove the chilled crust dough from the refrigerator.
2. In the bowl of a stand mixer, whip the cream cheese with the vanilla and powdered sugar until creamy.
3. Stir in the orange juice and orange zest and fold everything together.
4. In a separate bowl, whip the whipping cream until stiff peaks form. Fold it into the cream cheese mixture. Stir in the dissolved gelatin.
5. Pour the prepared mixture into the crust and smooth it out with a spatula.
6. Chill for about 4 hours before serving.
7. Cut into 8 slices and garnish with orange slices, chopped nuts, and/or whipped cream.

Nutrition per serving
Calories 487, fat 31.9 g, carbs 45.2 g, sugar 34.6 g,
Protein 6.7 g, sodium 346 mg

Strawberry and Lemonade Pie

Serves 8 | Prep time 20 minutes | Chill time 4 hours

Ingredients
1 recipe graham cracker crust (page 14)
1 (14-ounce) can sweetened condensed milk
1 cup freshly squeezed lemon juice
¼ cup powdered sugar
1 envelope powdered gelatin, dissolved in water
1 cup heavy whipping cream
1½ cups fresh strawberries

Directions
1. Remove the chilled crust dough from the refrigerator.
2. In a large mixing bowl, mix the sweetened condensed milk with the lemon juice.
3. Puree the strawberries until smooth and stir into the mixture along with the dissolved gelatin.
4. Whip the heavy whipping cream with the powdered sugar and gently fold it into the mixture.
5. Pour the prepared filling into the crust and refrigerate for about 4 hours.
6. Just before serving, decorate with some fresh strawberries on top.
7. Cut into 8 slices and serve.

Nutrition per serving
Calories 258, fat 11.1 g, carbs 35.4 g, sugar 33.4 g,
Protein 5.5 g, sodium 83 mg

Coconut Cream Pie

Serves 8 | Prep time 20 minutes | Chill time 4 hours

Ingredients
1 recipe graham cracker crust (page 14)
1 cup whole milk
2 packages instant coconut pudding
1 teaspoon vanilla extract
1½ cups heavy whipping cream
¼ cup powdered sugar
¼ cup toasted coconut flakes, for decoration

Directions
1. Remove the chilled crust dough from the refrigerator.
2. In a large mixing bowl, mix the whole milk with the coconut pudding and stir until combined.
3. Whip the heavy whipping cream with the powdered sugar and vanilla and gently fold it into the coconut mixture.
4. Pour the prepared filling into the crust and refrigerate for about 4 hours.
5. Just before serving, decorate with some toasted coconut on top.
6. Cut into 8 slices and serve.

Nutrition per serving
Calories 174, fat 11.9 g, carbs 14.8 g, sugar 6.3 g,
Protein 2.7 g, sodium 118 mg

Peanut Butter-Banana Icebox Pie

Serves 8 | Prep time 20 minutes | Chill time 4 hours

Ingredients
1 recipe graham cracker crust (page 14)
1½ cups heavy whipping cream, chilled
8 ounces cream cheese, softened
1 cup creamy peanut butter
½ cup light brown sugar
2 teaspoons vanilla extract
2 large bananas, sliced
Chocolate syrup, for decoration
½ heavy whipping cream, for decoration

Directions
1.   Remove the chilled crust dough from the refrigerator.
2.   In a large mixing bowl, beat the whipped cream until stiff peaks form.
3.   In another bowl, whip the cream cheese with peanut butter, light brown sugar, and vanilla.
4.   Gently fold the whipped cream into the peanut butter mixture.
5.   Pour the prepared filling into the crust and refrigerate for about 4 hours.
6.   Just before serving, decorate with whipped cream and banana slices and drizzle on some chocolate syrup.
7.   Cut into 8 pieces and serve.

Nutrition per serving
Calories 487, fat 38.3 g, carbs 29.4 g, sugar 19.4 g,
Protein 11.4 g, sodium 256 mg

Cranberry Pie

Serves 8 | Prep time 20 minutes | Chill time 4 hours

Ingredients
1 recipe graham cracker crust (page 14)
1½ cups heavy whipping cream
12 ounces cream cheese, softened
¼ cup light brown sugar
1 (14-ounce) can whole-berry cranberry sauce
1 teaspoon vanilla extract
Zest of 1 lemon
Fresh or frozen cranberries for garnish

Directions
1. Remove the chilled crust dough from the refrigerator.
2. In a large mixing bowl, whip the heavy whipping cream until stiff peaks form.
3. In another bowl, cream the cream cheese and light brown sugar together. Stir in the cranberry sauce and lemon zest and mix until combined.
4. Stir in the vanilla and gently fold in the whipped cream.
5. Pour the prepared filling into the crust and refrigerate for about 4 hours.
6. Just before serving, decorate with fresh or frozen cranberries on top.
7. Cut into 8 pieces and serve.

Nutrition per serving
Calories 334, fat 24.1 g, carbs 27.1 g, sugar 24.1 g,
Protein 3.9 g, sodium 156 mg

Grasshopper Pie

Serves 8 | Prep time 40 minutes | Chill time 4 hours

Ingredients
1 recipe graham cracker crust (page 14)
1½ cups heavy whipping cream
2½ cups cream (divided)
½ cup fresh mint leaves, roughly chopped
2 teaspoons gelatin, dissolved in water
½ teaspoon peppermint extract
½ cup powdered sugar
4 large egg yolks
1 drop green food coloring

Directions
1. Remove the chilled crust dough from the refrigerator.
2. In a saucepan over medium heat, bring 1½ cups of the cream and the mint leaves to a simmer.
3. Remove from heat, cover, and let steep for 30 minutes so the mint leaves can release their flavor.
4. Strain the mixture into the saucepan through a fine-mesh sieve.
5. Stir in the gelatin and bring to a simmer again.
6. In another bowl, add the egg yolks. Slowly pour in the hot cream mixture to temper the egg yolks, whisking constantly with a wire whisk. Stir in the green food coloring and peppermint extract. Let cool to room temperature.
7. Pour the prepared filling into the crust and refrigerate for about 4 hours.
8. Just before serving, whip the remaining cream with the powdered sugar and dollop on top of the pie.
9. Decorate with mint leaves.
10. Cut into 8 pieces and serve.

Nutrition per serving
Calories 180, fat 15.6 g, carbs 29.9 g, sugar 6.8 g
Protein 2.8 g, sodium 15 mg

Chocolate Caramel and Hazelnut Pie

Serves 8 | Prep time 20 minutes | Chill time 4 hours

Ingredients
1 recipe graham cracker crust (page 14)
8 ounces cream cheese, softened
½ cup Nutella
1 (7-ounce) jar marshmallow cream
1 cup heavy whipping cream
1 cup mini marshmallows
1 Snickers candy bar, chopped roughly, for decoration

Directions
1. Remove the chilled crust dough from the refrigerator.
2. In a large mixing bowl, beat the cream cheese with the Nutella and marshmallow cream.
3. In another bowl, whip the heavy whipping cream until stiff peaks form. Fold it into the Nutella and cream cheese mixture.
4. Pour the filling into the prepared crust and smooth it out.
5. Chill in the refrigerator for 4 hours before serving.
6. Just before serving, sprinkle the mini-marshmallows and chopped Snickers on top.

Nutrition per serving
Calories 452, fat 20.5 g, carbs 25.6 g, sugar 10.5 g
Protein 3.5 g, sodium 2.6 mg

Creamy Hazelnut Pie

Serves 8 | Prep time 20 minutes | Chill time 4 hours

Ingredients
1 recipe graham cracker crust (page 14)
8 ounces cream cheese, softened
1 cup icing sugar
1¼ cups Nutella, room temperature
8 ounces Cool Whip
¼ cup hazelnut spread

Directions
1. Remove the chilled crust dough from the refrigerator.
2. In a large mixing bowl, beat the cream cheese with the Nutella, hazelnut spread, and powdered sugar.
3. Gently fold the Cool Whip into the Nutella mixture until smooth.
4. Pour the filling into the prepared crust and smooth it out.
5. Chill in the refrigerator for 4 hours before serving.
6. Slice and serve.

Nutrition per serving
Calories 275, fat 19.6 g, carbs 18.6 g, sugar 20.3 g,
Protein 6.5 g, sodium 4.3 mg

Confetti Pie

Serves 8 | Prep time 20 minutes | Chill time 4 hours

Ingredients
1 recipe graham cracker crust (page 14)
1 pound cream cheese, softened
2 cups heavy whipping cream, chilled
2 teaspoons butter flavoring
1 teaspoon almond extract
1 cup icing sugar
½ cup assorted sprinkles

Directions
1. Remove the chilled crust dough from the refrigerator.
2. In a large mixing bowl, beat the cream cheese with the powdered sugar.
3. In another bowl, whip the heavy whipping cream until stiff peaks form. Fold into the cream cheese mixture.
4. Stir in the butter flavoring and almond extract and carefully fold in the sprinkles.
5. Pour the filling into the prepared crust.
6. Chill in the refrigerator for 4 hours before serving.
7. Slice and serve.

Nutrition per serving
Calories 567, fat 38.5 g, carbs 51.5 g, sugar 35.4 g,
Protein 6.4 g, sodium 396 mg

Caramel Pie

Serves 8 | Prep time 15 minutes | Cooking time 1 hour

Ingredients
1 recipe graham cracker crust (page 14)
Whipped cream, for topping

For the caramel
¾ cup sugar

For the custard
2 cups milk
3 egg yolks
4 tablespoons flour
¾ cup sugar
1 teaspoon vanilla extract
1 tablespoon unsalted butter
Pinch kosher salt

Directions
1. Remove the chilled crust dough from the refrigerator.
2. To make the caramel, cook the sugar in a saucepan over medium-low heat, stirring occasionally, until it is golden brown and caramelized (about 10 minutes). Keep it warm over very low heat.
3. To make the custard, in a saucepan, whisk the milk and egg yolks together.
4. Add the flour and sugar, and whisk until smooth.
5. Cook over medium heat, stirring constantly until the mixture thickens (about 10 minutes).
6. Add the caramelized sugar to the custard, whisking continuously until the mixture is smooth and thick (about 5 minutes).
7. Stir in the vanilla, butter, and salt.
8. To assemble, pour the custard into the crust.
9. Refrigerate until the filling is set (about 1 hour).
10. Serve topped with whipped cream topping.

Nutrition per serving
Calories 408, fat 22 g, carbs 49 g, sugar 33 g,
Protein 3 g, sodium 318 mg

Peanut Butter Crumble Pie

Serves 8 | Prep time 20–25 minutes

Ingredients
1 recipe graham cracker crust (page 14)

Crumbles
½ cup powdered sugar
¼ cup creamy peanut butter

Filling
5 ounces vanilla pudding mix
½ cup peanut butter
1 cup whipped cream
1 ½ cups milk

2 cups whipped cream for topping

Directions
1. Remove the chilled crust dough from the refrigerator.
2. In a medium bowl, whisk the peanut butter and sugar for the crumble mixture. (You can also use an electric mixer.)
3. Whisk until mixture appears crumbly, adding a few drops of water if needed.
4. Place half the crumble mixture in the crust.
5. In another medium bowl, whisk the pudding, peanut butter, and milk for 2 minutes.
6. Add in the cream and continue mixing.
7. Pour the filling mixture into the crust.
8. Add 1 cup of the whipped cream on top.
9. Pour the remaining crumble mixture in the crust and top with the remaining 1 cup of whipped cream.
10. Place in refrigerator for 10–12 hours or overnight.

Nutrition per serving
Calories 492, carbs 37g, fat 35g,
Protein 10g, sodium 341mg

Caramel Pecan Pie

Serves 6–8 | Prep time 25–30 minutes
Cooking time 5–10 minutes

Ingredients
1 recipe graham cracker crust (page 14)
28 caramels
1 envelope gelatin, unflavored
½ cup chopped pecans
Caramel ice cream topping
2 cups Cool Whip
½ cup cold water
1 teaspoon vanilla
1 cup milk
1 dash of salt

Directions
1. Remove the chilled crust dough from the refrigerator.
2. In a medium saucepan, combine the gelatin and water; wait for 1 minute.
3. Add in the milk, caramels, and salt.
4. Heat the pan over medium heat.
5. Refrigerate for 90–120 minutes.
6. Mix in the vanilla, Cool Whip, and pecans; combine well.
7. Pour the mixture into the crust.
8. Place it in the refrigerator for 10–12 hours or overnight.
9. Top with the ice cream (optional) and pecans; serve chilled!

Nutrition per serving
Calories 461, carbs 54g, fat 25g,
Protein 6g, sodium 278mg

Lemonade Icebox Pie

Serves 8 | Prep time 10 minutes

Ingredients
1 recipe graham cracker crust (page 14)
8 ounces cream cheese, softened
1 (14-ounce) can sweetened condensed milk
¾ cup lemonade concentrate, thawed
½ teaspoon vanilla extract
Pinch salt
8 ounces frozen whipped topping, thawed
2 drops yellow food coloring, optional
Lemon slices (well-drained) or zest for serving

Directions
1. Remove the chilled crust dough from the refrigerator.
2. In a mixing bowl, beat the cream cheese and sweetened condensed milk together until thoroughly combined.
3. Add the lemonade concentrate, vanilla, and salt. Mix well.
4. Fold in the whipped topping and food coloring, if using.
5. Spoon the pie filling into the crust and freeze until set.
6. Garnish with lemon slices or zest, and serve.

Nutrition per serving
Calories 422, fat 23 g, carbs 46 g, sugar 41 g,
Protein 7 g, sodium 267 mg

Chocolate Eggnog Pie

Serves 8 | Prep time 15 minutes | Cooking time 2 minutes

Ingredients
1 recipe graham cracker crust (page 14)
1 envelope unflavored gelatin
½ cup water, cold
⅓ cup sugar
2 tablespoons cornstarch
¼ teaspoon salt
2 cups eggnog
1½ squares unsweetened chocolate, melted
1 teaspoon vanilla
1 teaspoon rum extract
2 cups whipping cream
¼ cup confectioners' sugar

Directions
1. Remove the chilled crust dough from the refrigerator.
2. In a small bowl, soften the gelatin in the water. Set aside.
3. In a 1-qt. saucepan, combine the sugar, the cornstarch, and the salt. Gradually stir in the eggnog.
4. Cook over medium heat, stirring constantly until it has thickened.
5. Cook for 2 minutes. Remove from the heat and add the gelatin mixture, stirring until it is dissolved.
6. Divide the filling in half, setting half aside to cool.
7. Add the melted chocolate and the vanilla to half and stir well. Pour this mixture into the pie crust. Chill until set.
8. Add the rum extract to the remaining filling. Whip 1 cup of the cream and fold it into the cooled mixture. Spoon this over the chocolate layer and chill.
9. Whip the remaining cream and add the confectioners' sugar. Spread over the pie and garnish with the chocolate curls.

Nutrition per serving
Calories 268, fat 11 g, carbs 39 g, sugar 24 g,
Protein 5 g, sodium 182 mg

Strawberry Mousse Pie

Serves 8 | Prep time 15 minutes | Freezing time 15 minutes

Ingredients
Crust
7 ounces graham crackers, ground
Pinch of salt
2 tablespoons sugar
½ cup melted butter

Filling
1½ cups heavy whipping cream
1 teaspoon vanilla extract
3 tablespoons powdered sugar
2 cups fresh strawberries
2 tablespoons gelatin dissolved in water and melted over steam
½ cup fresh strawberries, diced, for serving

Directions
1. Combine the ground graham crackers, salt, sugar, and melted butter in a large bowl.
2. Transfer the mixture into a 13-inch pie pan and smooth it out to make an even pie crust.
3. Add the heavy cream to a bowl and whip it up with vanilla and powdered sugar.
4. Blitz the strawberries in a blender and pour them into the whipped cream.
5. Mix until fully combined and then stir in the dissolved gelatin.
6. Transfer the mixture into the pie crust and let it set in the freezer for 15–20 minutes.

Nutrition per serving
Calories 354, fat 25.2 g, carbs 30.4 g, sugar 14.7 g,
Protein 4.1 g, sodium 245 mg

Raspberry No-Bake Pie

Serves 8 | Prep time 10 minutes | Freezing time 20 minutes

Ingredients
For the crust
7 ounces ground graham crackers
Pinch of salt
2 tablespoons sugar
½ cup melted butter

For the filling
1½ cups heavy whipping cream
1 teaspoon vanilla extract
3 tablespoons powdered sugar
2 cups fresh raspberries
2 tablespoons gelatin dissolved in water and melted over steam
½ cup fresh raspberries diced for serving
2 tablespoons sprigs of mint

Directions
1. Place the ground graham crackers, salt, sugar, and melted butter in a bowl.
2. Mix until combined and press them down into a 10-inch pie dish.
3. Smooth it out with the help of a spatula.
4. In a bowl whip up the heavy whipping cream with the vanilla extract and powdered sugar.
5. Stir in the raspberries and add the melted gelatin to the mixture.
6. Pour the mixture into the pie pan and let the whole mixture freeze for 20 minutes.
7. Cut slices and serve with fresh raspberries and sprigs of mint.

Nutrition per serving
Calories 334, fat 22.5 g, carbs 31.4 g, sugar 14.1 g,
Protein 4.2 g, sodium 242 mg

RECIPE INDEX

APPENDIX

Cooking Conversion Charts

1. Measuring Equivalent Chart

Type	Imperial	Imperial	Metric
Weight	1 dry ounce		28g
	1 pound	16 dry ounces	0.45 kg
Vol-ume	1 teaspoon		5 ml
	1 dessert spoon	2 teaspoons	10 ml
	1 tablespoon	3 teaspoons	15 ml
	1 Australian tablespoon	4 teaspoons	20 ml
	1 fluid ounce	2 tablespoons	30 ml
	1 cup	16 table-spoons	240 ml
	1 cup	8 fluid ounces	240 ml
	1 pint	2 cups	470 ml
	1 quart	2 pints	0.95 l
	1 gallon	4 quarts	3.8 l
Length	1 inch		2.54 cm

Numbers are rounded to the closest equivalent

2. Oven Temperature Equivalent Chart

Fahrenheit (°F)	Celsius (°C)	Gas Mark
220	100	
225	110	1/4
250	120	½
275	140	1
300	150	2
325	160	3
350	180	4
375	190	5
400	200	6
425	220	7
450	230	8
475	250	9
500	260	

* Celsius (°C) = T (°F)-32] * 5/9
** Fahrenheit (°F) = T (°C) * 9/5 + 32
*** Numbers are rounded to the closest equivalent

Printed in Great Britain
by Amazon

26913047R00086